THE HEALING TOUCH OF MUSIC

the HEALING TOUCH of MUSIC:

AN EXPLORATION

ALANA WOODS

SOUND
VISTAS

ALBUQUERQUE, NEW MEXICO USA

Manufactured in the United States of America
Library of Congress Catalog Card Number: 2003098100

Woods, Alana, 1936–
The Healing Touch of Music: An Exploration
Includes index.
1. Music healing—psychological aspects. 2. Sound therapy
ISBN 0-9729049-1-3

First printing, 2003
Second printing, 2004

Cover photo: Jonathan Lowe
Cover and book design: Kathryn E. Campbell
Editor: Barbara Fandrich

SOUND
VISTAS

P. O. Box 20471
Albuquerque, NM 87154-0471

To my grandsons,

Gabriel and Benjamin

FOREWORD

It has been my pleasure to have known Alana Woods since the mid
1980s and to have had the privilege of sharing in and communicating
about the exciting discoveries and re-discoveries, as well as developments,
in the fields of sound healing and music healing that
she shares in this book. Her experiences are as varied as the researchers
and practitioners she presents to us. At the national "Music and
Health" conferences (1986, 1988, and 1990), and the College of Allied
Health seminars I hosted at Eastern Kentucky University, she
was both a participant and presenter. As can be heard on the CD
and read in the book, Alana Woods presents a case for the diversity
of methods, materials, and music that have in common the purpose
of utilizing music as sound for the facilitation of health.

The uses of prescriptive sound for health presented in *The Healing
Touch Of Music* represents three perspectives as represented by
the professions of 1) Music Therapy with the work of music therapist
Helen Bonny, Ph.D.; 2) Music Medicine with the work of the
French physician A. A. Tomatis, M.D.; and 3) Healing Music as created
by composers Steven Halpern, Don Campbell, Kay Gardner,
and Tom Kenyon, and the development of Vibroacoustic Healing
Sound Resources as created by Peter Kelly and Byron Eakin. Interwoven
throughout both the CD and the book are highlights of her
exploration and discovery of the many different approaches taken,
both in Western and non-Western cultures, to utilize the amazing
power of sound, appropriately organized and transmitted, to bring

healing, health, and wholeness.

Recognizing that her subtitle is "An Exploration," Alana Woods takes us with her on her own personal journey to discover and harness music for the purposes of healing. As well, she gives us insight into the journeys of other important figures on this road to establishing clarity as to why, what, and how the elements of sound, rhythm, melody, harmony, or form, when produced naturally, acoustically, or electronically, serve to affect our mind-brain-body systems for the ultimate purpose of remediating or preventing illness, or enhancing our wellness.

She recognizes that much can be learned from ancient approaches, as well as current methods and resources, and in exploring future trends and programs in the developing new science of music as it relates to healing. Her own musical life story is important in understanding the approach she took in exploring music as a healing force, and will resonate with many of the readers. While her intent was not to write a how-to guide book, she gives us many contacts and resources for us to explore, as well as general principles for us to use music and sound prescriptively. While some authors have made a conscious point of clarifying the distinction between sound as therapy and music as therapy, and rank them in a hierarchical order, Alana Woods clearly views both as important and valid approaches.

It is my hope that this book will provide the framework to lead you to explore more deeply this exciting topic. It has been my pleasure to have been an encourager in Alana Woods' learning journey, as well as a friend.

DR. ARTHUR HARVEY,

University of Hawaii at Manoa, October, 2003

CONTENTS

Foreword / 7

Contents / 9

Acknowledgments / 11

Introduction: A Personal Journey / 15

PART 1: BACKGROUND

CHAPTER 1   THE ANCIENT HERITAGE OF SOUND
AND MUSIC HEALING / 26

CHAPTER 2   HOLISTIC ORIENTATION OF MUSIC HEALING / 32

CHAPTER 3   THE EMOTIONAL RESONANCE OF MUSIC / 35

CHAPTER 4   PHYSIOLOGICAL EFFECTS OF MUSIC / 44

PART 2: THE MANY USES OF PRESCRIPTIVE SOUND

Introduction / 53

CHAPTER 5   THE BONNY METHOD: GUIDED IMAGERY
AND MUSIC (GIM) / 55

CHAPTER 6   THE TOMATIS METHOD:
AUDIO-PSYCHO-PHONOLOGY / 70

CHAPTER 7   THE BETAR INSTRUMENT / 84

CHAPTER 8   THE SOMATRON SOUND THERAPY TABLE / 94

CHAPTER 9   TOWARD A NEW SCIENCE OF MUSIC / 105

AFTERWORD / 113

APPENDIX 1   METHODS OF UTILIZING PRESCRIPTIVE SOUND / 115

APPENDIX 2   TONAL SYMBOLS OF INTUITIVE MUSIC / 118

APPENDIX 3   BODY RHYTHMS/PULSES / 120

APPENDIX 4   SOUND THERAPY QUESTIONNAIRE / 121

References / 123

Illustrations / 125

Index / 126

ACKNOWLEDGMENTS

I have had the great fortune to work with a wonderful, kind editor, Barbara Fandrich, who played a vital role in the editing and development of this book. Her clarity, steady support, and creative ideas have helped bring it all together.

I also wish to acknowledge Janie Johns, who first got me started on how to write a book; Dr. Lois Parker, who contacted me after reading my college thesis (from which this book originated), insisting it needed to be published as the information was valuable and should be read by students in this subject; and Helen Bonny, whose pioneering work gave me the key to open the first door to the memories of my deep connection to music and led me on to develop new ideas in depth.

My gratitude goes to all my teachers and mentors (visible and invisible) and friends who encouraged me: Tom Kenyon, Arthur Harvey, Maria McKinney, Joan Pritchard, Richard and Marilyn Rieger, Don Campbell, Gregg Braden, Renee Brodie, Betty Butler, Joel Andrews, Peter Kelly, Leslie Temple-Thurston, Pat Moffit Cook, Byron Eakin, Herb Ernst, and Werner John.

I am also grateful for the Muses who sing to me daily and for the valuable input from clients and audiences who have been my cocreators. To my friends and colleagues, thank you all for your friendship and support.

I Am Music

Servant and master am I; servant of those dead,
and master of those living.

Through me spirits immortal speak the message that
makes the world weep, and laugh, and wonder, and
worship.

I tell the story of love, the story of hate, the story that
saves and the story that damns.

I am the incense upon which prayers float to heaven. I
am the smoke which palls over the field of
battle where men lie dying with me on their lips. I
am close to the marriage altar, and when the graves
open I stand nearby.

I call the wanderer home, I rescue the soul from the
depths, I open the lips of lovers, and through me the dead
whisper to the living.

One I serve as I serve all; and the king I make my slave as
easily as I subject his slave.

I speak through the birds of the air, the insects of the
field, the crash of the waters on rock-ribbed shores,
the sighing of wind in the trees, and I am even heard by
the soul that knows me in the clatter of wheels on city
streets.

I know no brother, yet all men are my brothers; I am the
father of the best that is in them, and they are fathers of
the best that is in me; I am of them and they are of me.
For I am an instrument of God.

ANONYMOUS

INTRODUCTION:

A Personal Journey

*Our ultimate destiny is to re-connect with our essential Being
and express from an extraordinary, divine reality in the
ordinary physical world, moment by moment.*

ECHART TOLLE

In order to properly research and understand the use of sound and music in healing, one would need to be many things: physician, historian, philosopher, brain physicist, linguist, bioenergist, music therapist, psychoacoustician, audiologist, musicologist, psychiatrist, and psychologist!

Fortunately, to use music as a complement to the healing process, one just needs to become quiet and aware.

I remember coming home from school one Friday afternoon when I was in the fifth grade. It had been a long, tiring day and I was the last one on the school bus at the end of the run. I wearily stepped off onto the gravel at the end of our driveway, glad to be home again, with the weekend coming up. But my good feelings didn't last long, as I suddenly felt a foreboding as I neared the house. The vacuum sweeper was running, and this meant my mother would be in an angry mood. Softly I tuned my mind to a certain place where there was the sound of lovely symphony music. This calmed and supported me, offering a healing balm as I walked into the house. This was the first time I was aware I had actually been hearing various types of music in my mind all of my life.

Perhaps you, too, hear music in your mind or are humming a little tune during the day. You might not be aware that the music has influenced your mood or triggered a specific memory, no matter where the music comes from. One of the most poignant melodies is the sound of "taps" being played by a bugle at military funerals. Most people in the United States have heard this haunting melody that usually brings tears to the eyes.[1]

Quite often people are unaware it is music that has influenced their mood or triggered a specific memory. Think for a moment of a sports event you may have attended when bands were playing a march, or movies you may have watched when very dramatic scenes were portrayed. Certain emotions were evoked. These are the effects of music.

Around 1975 I was given a book and audiotape that opened new doorways in my understanding of the effects of music. The book, *Music and Your Mind: Listening with a New Consciousness* (Bonny and Savory 1973), tells of expanded experiences bringing moments of insight, creativity, self-realization, and spiritual experiences. These experiences were triggered while listening to special music in a certain way.

Trained as a music therapist, musician, and psychotherapist, Bonny developed a pioneer model of psychotherapy with music. Known today as Guided Imagery and Music (GIM), Bonny's method is discussed in greater detail in Chapter 5.

The audiotape I received likewise expanded my understanding.

---

[1] This special melody began in 1862 during the Civil War when a young Confederate soldier died in battle, and a paper with music notes and words was found in his pocket by his father, a Union captain, who was also on that battlefield and didn't know his son had enlisted. This melody, played on a bugle, is still used today.

Snowflakes Are Dancing is a musical recording by an artist known as Tomita, who received an award for his expertise in synthesized music in the mid-1970s.

Listening to this tape for the first time, I experienced extraordinary expanded awareness. Visually, I perceived intense color forms and images of a panorama of the world. I marvel at the synchronicity of being handed the book and tape at the same moment. There are no accidents in the events of our lives!

The ideas in Bonny's book *Music and Your Mind* have greatly influenced my life and my practice as a musician and healing arts practitioner. My childhood memories of the many times I had used music to heal my emotions were rekindled, and those experienced memories have greatly informed my practice.

As a child I played the piano for fifteen years. Starting at the age of four, my mother actually made me sit at the piano to practice every day. I did not have a day off, not even during summer. I did not like this discipline, but now I am very grateful. I learned music structures very well and at an early age.

Although I had only one teacher during most of my training, I also studied at the Conservatory of Music in Kansas City, Missouri, with Arthur Rubenstein's sister-in-law, who taught me how to play the music of Chopin, and suggested I go onto the concert stage. At the age of thirteen I played a solo piano concert that required the memorization of twenty-three pieces of music. Later I learned to play improvisational music, inspired by melodies in the moment.

My piano was situated before a large picture window overlooking a beautiful nature scene: tall pine trees, birds, the bounty of life. I would often sit and play for hours, letting the music tell the story of my life. Music transported me, healed me. I would leave the piano peaceful yet energized, envisioning each note in unison with the invigorating rhythms of nature laid out before me. Years later when I was studying to be a harpist, my teacher told me to practice with the harp in front of a window with a beautiful nature scene, as it would help give phrasing to the music.

Later, when I was in my early twenties, I would drive my convertible into the countryside on beautiful summer mornings, listening to the car radio as the trees and grasses passed beside me. I would feel transported to another world by the symphonies I heard. And these symphonies were not limited to the radio! Through nature I heard all of earth's creatures as music-makers: the singing of ants and spiders, the whistle of termites, the scream of flies, the babbling of streams, and the moaning of the wind. Music would bring tears to my eyes, music would urge me to sing along with it, and music would clothe my moods with comfort and definition, expressing what I could not put into words. I have since learned many other sounds are music, sounds such as speaking, breathing, silence.

Throughout my life, music has helped restore me spiritually, psychologically, and physically. For example, music enabled me to overcome my fear of dentistry. It helped heal an arthritic condition that had started in my hand. It helped establish a flow of creativity in my work as an artist, and brought a valuable addition to church members through my ministry work. And, most uplifting, it has helped me in times of great loneliness.

The influence of Bonny's work on my life and my work cannot be overstated. To grow as a music practitioner and to greater understand the concepts and methodology behind Guided Imagery and Music, I contacted Bonny in 1978. She was working in Baltimore, Maryland, at the time and I arranged to study with her.

I made many trips in the next several years to complete a series of training in Phases I and II of Bonny's method. With this solid and meaningful background, I then began to reach out, expanding my understanding by studying with other pioneers in subjects related to music and healing.

For more than fifteen years I followed an evolving and enriching educational path that included studies in brain physiology (music and brain states), psychology, hypnotherapy, imagery, art/drawing interpretation, education, and psychoacoustics. I then began to set up my own experiments with music, researching its emotive and healing properties.

My subjects included mentally retarded children and adults, Alzheimer's patients, hospice patients in a center for dying, and other seriously ill adults and children. I also spent one month working with patients in a state mental institution. In my regular practice I worked with private clients and workshop audiences. All these settings and experiences confirmed for me the validity of using prescriptive sound in healing.

As part of my field studies, I carried a Celtic harp into hospitals, schools, and nursing homes, playing music for children as well as the dying, and many others. I also used different selections of recorded music. I told stories with the harp, creating an hour called *Musical Tales for the Inner Being,* tales of transformation, for children as well as adults.

I discovered the combination of storytelling with the harp was a very potent healing art form. I remember one evening at a Unity church in Florida where I asked my audience to move their chairs into a circle. With the ceiling lights dimmed and one lamp over the harp, I told my stories. At the end of the hour, there was silence. No one spoke or moved. Finally I asked, "How are you feeling?"

One by one people related memories that had surfaced. "I've never experienced anything like this before," said one participant. One woman related that her wonderful mother had recently died, and one of the stories I had told was of wise women of which, the woman said, her mother was one. Another woman remembered her childhood home and how she used to sit with her grandfather near a lily pond in the backyard. He would tell her stories as they watched dragonflies and frogs. Tears were shed quietly and there was a great feeling of comfort and peace in the room.

In the winter of 1988 I had an opportunity to go to Asia with Don Campbell, Kay Gardner, and a group of musicians to hear its music and its sounds. The trip enabled me to listen in a new way, a way not often taught in Western culture.

We traveled to Ubud, the center of the island of Bali (a small island at the tip of Java), and one of the 13,000 islands that comprise Indonesia. Both Java and Bali are famous for their gamelan music and dance, and Ubud is the center of the arts in Bali.

The essence of gamelan music is timelessness. There are few climaxes and resolutions, or contrasts of loudness and softness. The listener is thus free to move in and out of the music. (This is an objective of Western minimalist music, such as that produced by Windham Hill recordings or the compositions of Philip Glass and Steve Reich.)

In Ubud I took some lessons on a native instrument commonly known as a *tingklik*. It can be found in many Balinese households and is played by the children and adults. It is comprised of eleven or twelve bamboo tubes suspended on a wooden form. It is played like a xylophone using long sticks with rubber discs at the ends. The tingklik has a soft, hollow, percussive sound, like the tinkling of raindrops on a roof. An incredible tuning happens in the body while playing this instrument. It is the same form of tuning that occurs when the body is dancing, moving to Balinese music. The repetitive rhythm of sound and movement of music sequences creates a wonderful balanced feeling in the body.

Bali gave me a sense of wholeness and completeness. I walked the streets of Asia, ate the food, slept in its rooms, exchanged conversation with local people, and celebrated the culture by participating in the gamelan orchestra and Balinese dance through classes with master teachers of the island. As I engaged in the constant banter of buying and selling goods (which is extremely active and requires one to learn the art of negotiation), I found my heartbeat naturally took up the cadence of my surroundings.

My roots in humanity felt stronger as I joined in the inner weavings of a people who openly shared aspects of both the light and the dark side in their daily music performances and other rituals. There was the constant singing and laughter of children, monkeys chattering, and roosters crowing, from early morning into the night. I heard the same rhythms of these activities repeated in the music of the gamelan orchestra.

As I continued my studies in Eastern methods of healing with music I was most interested in cross-cultural methodologies, and sought to discover how these cultures differ in their approach to therapeutic sound.

In 1990 I spent a month in Greece, teaching two weeks on the island of Skyros. My classes were held at Skyros Institute, a European holistic institute. I taught two courses: "The Healing Touch of Music" and "The Secret of Healing through the Arts," in which I taught the use of the mandala and spontaneous drawings. I was awakened each morning by the sounds of thousands of birds, including roosters, and tinkling bells from herds of sheep. The experience was delightful.

In the latter part of my journey I visited ruins from the fourth century, meditating at the oracle at one of the temples and pondering the idea that Paracelsus had given "music prescriptions" to his patients for both mental and physical disorders (Tame 1984, 156). What a profound idea! I was impressed by this and remembered it for later use.

In 1996 I was invited to join a group of fellow musicians to travel to India, under the guidance of Pat Moffit Cook. Cook is a researcher in cross-cultural healing with music. We attended music concerts at night, sitting on top of a building under the stars, and looking down on the performances. We visited a healer who used his voice to sing and chant in a healing ritual at a small village outside Bombay.

In Bombay we took a boat to an island to visit the Ajanta and Alora caves. These sacred caves were carved by hand over a period of 150 years. They date back to the fourth century B.C. The caves are divided into long, narrow rooms, each with a giant Buddha seated at the end and high curved ceilings with round arches every few feet. The floors of the cave are smooth and feel cool to bare feet.

The rooms of the caves are lighted naturally by the opening at each cave's entrance, and this light is artificially boosted by reflected light from large, round metal discs held by the guides who accompanied us. The guides tilt the mirrored surface of each disc so sunlight from the cave opening streams a golden beam onto the statue, lending light to the chamber. Tall, heavy, wooden doors close off the entrance to the rooms, enhancing the acoustics. Once the doors closed, our group began single-tone chanting.

My experiences in the Ajanta and Alora caves confirmed for me the therapeutic and healing stimulus of sound. Harmonics and overtones flowed with beautiful resonance through the chambers … gathering strength and power as our voices rose in a single tone. I was transported to another world … a world of ancient times and ancient sounds when monks lived here and walked through these same halls, chanting their own songs. Perhaps some still do.

Music rituals can be found throughout India. My group, for example, listened entranced as an Indian man chanted in deep tones in the ethereal beauty of the Taj Mahal, a structure noted for its resonance. We chanted with hundreds of Indian people at the ashram of the late teacher, Sai Baba of Shiridi, who had passed on many years before. The feeling at the ashram was deeply still and sacred.

These personal experiences of nature and music, together with my research and travels, helped me construct my theory of how sound relates to nature and how we draw from its inspiration and healing. I continued my comparative studies of sound, music, and healing, working for many years toning in caves outside Santa Fe, New Mexico. It was here that I more fully developed my understanding of the effects of sound.[2]

I have related the major events which can influence and increase a personal understanding of music: a great interest in sound during childhood, sensitive attunement with nature, understanding about consciousness and music, and studies of world music and sound. In the following chapters we will explore how these influences can support healing.

---

[2] Some of that work was recorded and includes a toning session I did with a terminally-ill woman. My video *The Sound of Healing* describes that work and shows those experiences in greater detail.

PART 1

Background

CHAPTER 1

The Ancient Heritage of Sound and Music Healing

It would seem that there was never a time when music did not exist, and when the fundamental urge and feelings of man were not expressed through it. But even without man's participation, music fills the earth.

EDGAR CAYCE

The roots of healing through music evolved from ancient knowledge. The ancients knew far more than we do today about the nature of sound and how music can be used to integrate, harmonize, and heal. Ancient Hindus, Tibetan Buddhists, and Mayans recognized that each person has his or her own "resonating frequency" that, when sounded, could return an ailing individual to internal harmony.

As stated in the book *The Healing Forces of Music* by Randall McClellan (p. 110-111): "It is possible the use of music or sound for healing could have originated more than thirty thousand years ago, at a time when illness was a great mystery." Illness was thought to have been caused by an evil spirit that needed to be extracted from the mind or body of the ill person. The earliest attempt to do this was possibly the wailing sounds made by a group of villagers who would form a circle around the ill person. They would chant or make sounds for hours at a time. Later, gourd rattles and drums were added. Sound was used as a vehicle for incantation, and calling forth various deities. Much later, as history progressed, it was through the work of India, Egypt, Greece, and Rome that music was used as a form of therapy.

The concept of music as a healing force began with one philosophical concept held in common by shaman, priests, and ancient prophets: all that is manifested has a complementary non-manifested form at its source.

The sound of music, according to this philosophy, represents a microcosm of the order of the universe: the movement of galaxies, stars, planets, sun and moon; the cycle of seasons, days, nights, ocean tides, and the birth and death of all cellular life.

A system relating music sounds to the order of the universe was developed as early as the third century B.C. In today's world all one has to do is listen to or practice music to better understand these universal harmonies, experience their fluidity, and let them teach how to flow with life.

Hebrew and Greek ancients also knew of the healing properties of music. King Saul's insanity was reputedly cured overnight by the power of David's harp. In the Greek epic *The Odyssey,* the flow of blood from the wounds of Ulysses is stopped by the singing of Autolycus.

The ancient Greek scientist, Pythagoras,[3] helped his disciples calm their minds in the evening by playing music for them that produced deep sleep and prophetic dreams. In the morning a song might have been sung in order to protect one from epidemics.

---

[3]Pythagoras of Samos (circa 580–500 B.C.), the Greek mathematician, was founder of the Pythagorean school of philosophy and brotherhood in Crotona, Italy. He is credited with developing the Western music scale by calculating intervals based on the harmonic series (this system was an ancient predecessor of our current equal temperament scale). From *Harp Therapy Journal,* 1996,vol.1:2, back page.

Pythagoras believed that reality, at its deepest level, is mathematical in nature. He saw the importance of harmonious soul development, and believed in reincarnation. In his training of novitiates, a vow of silence was the rule, except when speaking with the master. The seven musical modes were studied and used prescriptively. For example, in the morning certain modes were used to cleanse the mind from sleep. In the evening, modes were played to soothe and relax.

Pythagoras preferred stringed instruments, especially the seven-string lyre, which he thought was an echo of the celestial bodies. The body of the lyre symbolized the human form; the strings were the nerves. When played, the spirit would create harmony. Pythagoras's school formed a link between the Egyptian mystery schools and the development of Greek and European philosophies.

We do not know much about the structure of the music of the ancient world, as there is no notated music available prior to 100 B.C. in Greece and 500 B.C. in China. There are drawings and writings, figures playing instruments on the walls of buildings, and the music of India is said to be three thousand years old, but written music did not evolve until much later.

When I was in Greece, I walked around in temples and went out into the countryside with two Greek women I met who gifted me with a drive to a temple where there were no tourists, several hours outside Athens. I walked through the crumbling temple and out into the woods where an oracle well was in evidence. As I sat beside it I envisioned the scene that had been in ancient days.

Epidaurus, a city of ancient Greece, was a center of healing where people would gather to spend several days or weeks in holistic care (Houston, 1987).

After settling into one of the many guest houses of the city, they would walk the streets to view the temples. They would enter some to offer prayers in hopes of evoking the Olympian gods. Perhaps they would watch high drama in the surrounding magnificent marble theaters, venues that featured perfect acoustics. There they would find comedies with ribald themes, with the actors often dressed in ridiculous costumes.

In these theaters they would experience a gamut of emotions from terror to suspense and laughter. They might take herbal baths or massages, laugh in the "house of comedians," and then go to one of the local physicians later in the day. The doctor would give both spiritual and medical guidance.

At night, they would sleep in rooms filled with incense of pine and the rhythm of quietly chanted prayers. The following week, they might do some exercises in a gymnasium or listen to music in concert halls. Finally, with sufficient preparation, they would be given a bath in the sea by one of the priests, and amid incense and prayers would prepare to enter the beautiful Temple of Asclepius.

The great Temple of Asclepius, built in honor of Asclepius, the god of Nootherapeia, or mind healing, was the center for healing rituals. A background of powerful music and chanting was in this place. There they would ask the priests for a vision of meaning showing them the sorrow which had made them ill. These priests recounted inspiring stories of how others had been healed miraculously, and thus faith in their healing powers increased.

In the evening they would dress in white tunics and join the other patients in special rooms where healing dreams were given. During the night, priests and priestesses walked among the ill, putting ointments on the diseased parts. Serpents and dogs would then lick these parts. Patients fell asleep to beautiful music and dreamed magnificent dreams where it seemed the god Asclepius himself stood before them and healed them.

In the morning, there would be immense rejoicing and celebration for the healings in the night. Some would have been healed, others would feel better in mind and body, and most would have had a dream of significance for their life. The priests helped interpret the dreams and affirmed the healings.

There was an enormous richness and variety of experience in the ritual of healing in Greece. The healing centers of Asclepius spread throughout Greece, Egypt, and Rome. The fullest flowering of these was found at Epidaurus. The people who made the pilgrimage to the sacred temples of Asclepius experienced a quickening of the total person through art, music, dance, drama, healing therapy, sacred practice, laughter, altered states of consciousness, and archetypal realities.

Music has a power that cannot be denied. It acts simultaneously on the mind and the senses and blends ideas and emotions into a flow of harmony and balance, if the appropriate type is used. The spirit cannot become full, the body radiantly healthy, without the deep feelings of beauty and life found in the fullest use of the senses. Many people are unable to open themselves sufficiently to this experience. Then music becomes a bridge, for it can evoke deep responses that open our emotional capacity.

As we will discover in Chapters 3 and 4, exciting studies about the human brain show there are many more important connections to our life through the environment of sound than was previously thought. Not only are we continually surrounded and influenced by sounds at every moment, waking or sleeping, but many of these sounds are incoherent, cacophonous, and damaging. Studies show

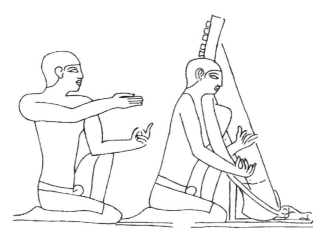

Harpist and chironomist, 5ᵗʰ Dynasty

that those who live in big cities with heavy traffic and the many electrical waves in the air, have a greater chance of becoming ill. Evidence shows that an antidote is merely spending more time with nature and her sounds, away from the busy streets. The immune system is enhanced when the body is coherent, flowing smoothly. Music engages the whole body as well as the brain, and there is a healing quality to it.

Music has long been known to serve a wonderful adjunct to all therapies and wellness disciplines. When the deeper systems of the body are in harmony, we can relax and be in the natural flow with our system. Music contributes—and always has contributed—much to the healing of the world. In music lies the power to complete the great circle of the evolution of human consciousness.

CHAPTER 2

Holistic Orientation
of Music Healing

All these musical compositions have definite effects
on the circulation of the blood in the brain as well
as other parts of the body ... [with] proven value
to restore us as potently as many drugs.
And these music tonics leave no ill after-effect.

EDWARD PODOLSKY, M.D., 1935

In *The Search for the Beloved*, Houston suggests there is a great need for a global Ascelepian for our time. The ancient Greek methods are reflected today in the many holistic healing centers that are successful in treating the many aspects of the patient who comes for healing of mind and body.

The American Holistic Medical Association was founded in 1978. The holistic approach to health is a much different model from the existing form of traditional medicine most widely practiced in Western cultures today. Whereas traditional methods are curatively oriented, holistic approaches tend to emphasize preventative, proactive care.

Holistic medicine addresses the whole person. It integrates alternative and conventional therapies to promote optimum health, and includes an analysis of the patient's physical and emotional well being, lifestyle, and environment. As an added element, the patient learns how to participate in his/her own healing process.

Health, according to traditional medicine, means ongoing medical attention, rather than allowing patients to learn responsibility in health care. Specifically, illness in this model is generally regarded as a complaint to be eliminated rather than a condition which can, in itself, provide insights and opportunities for self-discovery, getting to the real cause of the illness. In the holistic view, illness is seen as a messenger, or indication that aspects of the life are out of harmony.

The early priest-healers of Greece would be dismayed if they walked through our treatment centers today (hospitals) and observed that particular medicines are recommended as treatment for specific diseases on a general basis (for example, aspirin or aspirin substitute is prescribed for most all cases of headache). In the holistic Greek model, treatment prescriptions were tailored for individual requirements.

The word holistic comes from the Greek *holos* which means whole, and from it we derive our English words, holy, whole, and health, and even the greeting "hello," which means "May you have good health."

Plato was an advocate of the holistic approach to health saying:

The cure of the part should not be attempted without treatment of the whole. No attempt should be made to cure the body without the soul, and if the head and body are to be healthy you must begin by curing the mind, for this is the great error of our day in the treatment of the human body, that Physicians first separate the soul from the body.

It is amazing that these are the very same insights that are guiding the shift in healthcare practice today.

What is meant by the word disease? According to *Merriam-Webster's Collegiate Dictionary*, Tenth Edition: "Disease is a condition of the living animal or plant body or of one of its parts that impairs normal functioning; sickness; malady; trouble." Quite literally, it is dis-ease.

For our understanding, the definition of disease in the holistic view must also include not just the body, but also the mind and emotions. For what we think and feel does affect the physical body. I have been inspired by what Byron Katie says in her book, *Loving What Is* (Katie 2002). Bodies don't think, care, or have any problem with themselves, they never beat themselves up or shame themselves. They simply try to keep themselves balanced and to heal themselves. They are entirely efficient, intelligent, kind, and resourceful.

In *Stalking the Wild Pendulum*, Bentov suggests we look at disease as out-of-tune behavior of the body. He includes both mind and body as aspects of health. The application of harmonious vibrations will cause the body to be in tune again.

The use of sound to assist us to become in tune is the basic principle of healing with sound and music, and seen as a holistic way of healing.

CHAPTER 3

The Emotional
Resonance of Music

*It is music's lofty mission to shed light
on the depths of the human heart.*

ROBERT SCHUMANN

"Harmonizing vibrations" can be either of sound or music. Sound healing treats the body first, using resonance (as in a frequency resonance such as drum rhythms, without harmony). Music healing treats the mind and emotions first, then affects the body through resonance.

The determination of whether a sound is "music" or just "sound" has cultural bias. For instance, Middle Eastern music may seem more like "sound" to the Western ear because it has different music intervals and intonations from those commonly heard in the West. But, on closer examination, we discover that Eastern music may be distinguished from sound because it has meaning and purpose for the listener.

The music experience may be categorized by a range of qualities. Standing alone, each of these qualities is indeed a characteristic of sound; however, it is the varied combinations of these qualities that distinguish music from sound. These qualities include:

- **Rhythm** (periodic pulsation)—Variations in tempo (speed), meter (groupings/accent), nature of subdivision (simple/compound), complexity

- **Melody** (linear/horizontal expression)—Variations in smooth or angular, tonal or non-tonal, speed, balance, structure

- **Harmony** (simultaneous soundings of pitch/vertical)— Variations in simple or complex, dissonant or consonant

- **Form**—Variations in structural symmetry or asymmetry, balance between unity and variety, simple or complex

- **Tempo**—Relationship between pulse or music and metabolic pulse

- **Volume** (amplitude)—Variations in decibel level

- **Orchestration** (timbre)—Variations in number and type of instruments used

- **Reproduction**—Variations in quality of sound

In order to understand the meaning of the beat or pulse of a piece of music, we have to merge with the music, experience how it moves us kinesthetically, not intellectually. When the music begins, the body listens. As you listen to a piece of music ask yourself: How does it make me feel? How does it affect my breathing?

This form of listening is supported scientifically. When two or more oscillators in the same field are pulsing at nearly the same time they tend to "lock in" and begin pulsing at exactly the same rate. Yet the body reacts to music in ways far greater than the kinesthetic; the emotive power of music is in itself far-reaching in its ability to affect mind, body, and soul.

Music is a language of the emotions, as well as one of its direct expressions. How music communicates to the emotions can be scientifically measured and has been researched by Manfred Clynes and Kate Hevner.

Clynes, a concert pianist, inventor and neurophysiologist, has shown emotions exist in their own right as potential patterns in the nervous system and can be triggered by music, independent of specific associations with people or events. For each emotion, there is an innate brain program which gives a shape for all expressions of that emotion. Clynes has shown emotions exist in their own right as potential patterns in the nervous system and can be triggered by music, independent of specific associations with people or events.

Composers are able to tap into what Clynes calls "sentic forms," basic emotional shapes that relate to feelings. In his book *Sentics: The Touch of Emotions,* Clynes identifies what he calls the standard cycle of emotions in graphic form, in the drawings below:

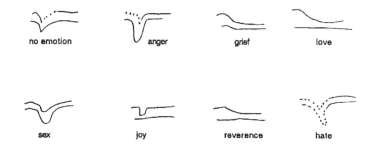

These drawings represent the shape of "pulse" which determines the subtle character of music, the "soul of the music."

In 1937, Hevner identified sixty-six adjectives in eight related groups of evoked emotions to music. The eight groups of adjectives are arranged around an imaginary circle so that one group is related to and compatible with each one, side by side. Adjacent groups have common characteristics and groups at diagonally opposite points of the circle are unlike each other. The complete circle involves a wide range of the most common affective experiences.

Today we use various adjectives to define mood states depicted in music. These different mood states have underlying emotional patterns.

```
                                6
                              merry
                 7            joyous           5
              exhilarated     gay           humorous
              soaring         happy         playful
              triumphant      cheerful      whimsical
              dramatic        bright        fanciful         4
              passionate                    quaint        lyrical
              sensational                   sprightly     leisurely
      8       agitated                      delicate      satisfying
  vigorous    exciting                      light         serene
  robust      impetuous                     graceful      tranquil
  emphatic    restless                                    quiet
  martial                                       3         soothing
  ponderous                                 dreamy
  majestic                                  yielding
  exalting       1                 2        tender
             spiritual         pathetic     sentimental
             lofty             doleful      longing
             awe-inspiring     sad          yearning
             dignified         mournful     pleading
             sacred            tragic       plaintive
             solemn            melancholy
             sober             frustrated
             serious           depressing
                               gloomy
                               heavy
                               dark
```

Arrangement of adjectives for recording the mood effect of music.

In ancient Athens, Plato and Aristotle spoke of the effect of specific modes, one of which (the Lydian Mode) would bring on aggressive emotional states, which were forbidden at that time.

There is now a much broader understanding about the relationship between the body and emotions today. Fresh insights into why certain alternative treatments work with some people, and not with others, have come to light through the research of Valerie Hunt, Director of the Bioenergy Fields Foundation and professor emeritus from the Department of Physiological Sciences at the University of California at Los Angeles. Hunt has made unique and groundbreaking contributions to a new and scientific model of human behavior physiology, with important practical implications.

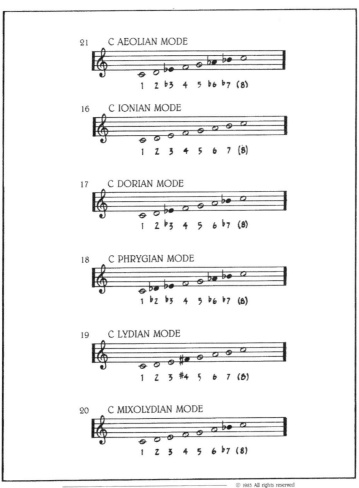

· P.D. COSTELLO PUBLICATIONS · P.O. BOX 8132. SANTA CRUZ · CA · 95061

Six Greek Modes

According to Hunt, there are three levels of emotional intelligence or instructions:[4]

- **Tissue level**—instructions to cells about living, growing multiplying, dying. The memories would be about cell injuries, and good or bad experiences. *Treatment:* Massage is effective for this level, as well as touch, joint manipulation, exercise, acupuncture.

- **Brain level**—primary control systems and organs, causing digestive, urinary, and breathing malfunctions. This level can override the genes. Memories of life experiences are stored and colored by family and belief systems. *Treatment:* Neurolinguistic programming, meditation, group therapy, guided imagery, the arts, music, writing, drama, storytelling, exercise systems—all involving the person's participation.

- **Highest levels of consciousness (the psyche)**—Here emotional blocks are the most stubborn and persistent. This includes past life memory and experiences where the person was in an altered state during major trauma. These memories are not available to everyday recall and one must return to an altered state to retrieve them. These emotions are intense and overshadow those of the brain or tissue level. These blocks are directly associated with major wasting diseases such as ALS, Multiple Sclerosis, and cancer. *Treatment:* Hypnosis, free association, spiritual expression, prayer, art, music, poetry, shamanistic ritual, dedicated meditation.

Emotions give the body instructions, and direct feelings and thoughts about reality. Each person builds his or her unique emotional program from what is important to him or her. How we perceived sounds we heard in early childhood, for instance, informs our

---

[4] Permission was given to use material from Hunt's Web site www.bioenergyfields.org.

emotional connections. Memories of life experiences are stored and colored also by the family and cultural belief systems. In *Molecules of Emotion: The Science Behind Mind-Body Medicine* (Pert 1999), the author states that genes also have memory and emotion.

We live in a landscape of familiar sounds. In my workshops, "The Healing Touch of Music," which I conducted several years ago, I would ask participants this question: "What were the sounds you heard when you were a child?" One woman related how she had grown up in New York City, so the first sounds she heard in the morning were of traffic, including big trucks, taxis, and buses. In fact, these sounds were a continual comfort in the background of her life. Another woman remembered there had been a train track running the property line of her back yard. Trains passed through every afternoon with their familiar rumbles, clangs, and squeaks. Another student said the first sounds she heard were her father yelling!

I spent the first twenty years of my life on a farm in the Midwest. I remember wakening each morning to birdsongs, soon followed by roosters crowing, cows mooing and a general hubbub of activity. But it's always the birdsongs that sound first through the mist of my dreams. In my half-awake state I would listen, thrilled by their symphony. I learned a lot from these little birds, their constant tonal vibrations in the upper ranges as high as one could hear. What gentle, coherent energy! Memories of life experiences such as these are stored and then colored by our family and cultural belief systems.

One music therapy model employs music that helps the patient become entrained with it. This principle is known as the Alschuller/ Iso principle: matching music to mood. It is not based on what a person likes or dislikes, but what resonates within him or her at the moment.

Careful evaluation is made with the subject to begin to access the mood state, then the therapist selects music that will match this mood as closely as possible. What is soothing and harmonious to one person may be the opposite for another. Dormant fields of disturbance deep within the unconscious mind may be triggered and released.

The universal power of music to elicit unconscious feelings has prompted one writer to describe music as the "beautiful disturber" (Rosenfeld 1985, 48–56).

I once worked with a client, who, during one of our sound therapy sessions, experienced a deeper insight into her marriage than she had ever been able to see before. She said:

> I see myself standing in front of me, then I see the man I'm married to. He is open and receptive. Now I understand! I am the one that is blocked, not my husband. For ten years I haven't let him get close enough. I've held him at arm's length. I can see I have been wanting people to express themselves in certain ways. This control issue has got to go.

As a practitioner or therapist, it is vital to remember the health of a patient comes when there is freedom to process energies effectively on all levels. The body can repair itself and regenerate itself beyond what we can even imagine if the blocks to the emotional energy systems are removed.

In my own experience I have discovered that a key to opening up the deep memories is deep relaxation through music. Music helps facilitate the transition from awareness of our place in the outer world to a deeper understanding of our inner selves. To find the right sound, however, the right music must be selected, and each person must be instructed on how to work with it.

Working with a woman who was terminally ill with cancer brought insight to my practice. This woman was undergoing chemotherapy treatments that were closing down her throat and weakening her lungs. I selected for her music that was open and soothing.[5] At the end of her session she said her stomach felt relaxed for the first time in months, and her breathing had opened up. Later she said her experience during our session had given her insight about her relationship in the world and her need to be more trusting, open, and committed. She said she had been given this message: "Let go and turn your face to the light. It's not going to be easy, but it is easier than to slide into death."

---

[5] The music "Wave Form," by Tom Kenyon, Acoustic Brain Research, was played.

CHAPTER 4

Physiological Effects of Music

Music does produce effects by feeding us stimuli
through many channels at one time.

D. B. FRY, PH.D.

Most studies of music's effect on mind and body concern physiology: pulse rate, blood pressure, metabolism, respiration, galvanic skin response, chemical and hormonal levels, pain perception threshold, memory function, and motor coordination. In music therapy training students learn numerous uses of music to enhance learning. Only recently has there been interest, knowledge, and understanding of the link between music and the brain.

We know, through scientifically documented research and experience, that there are specific physiological, neurological, and psychological changes that take place through the application of music:[6]

PHYSIOLOGICAL:

- Breathing rate change
- Pulse rate change
- Blood pressure change

---

[6]Notes from Dr. Arthur Harvey's workshop, "Music and the Brain," Eastern Kentucky University, 1987.

- Pupillary response
- Muscle tone change
- Blood flow
- Modified cellular resonance
- Modified vibrational processes

PSYCHOLOGICAL:

- Mood change
- Altered states produced in imagery
- Cathartic process
- Non-verbal communication
- Objectified subject reality
- Neurological:
- Modified brain wave functioning
- Activated neurotransmitters
- Enhanced psychoneuroimmunology

As we discovered in Chapter 3, sound can assist us to become literally in tune, and this is the basic principle of healing with sound and music.

In order to explain this in tune state, let us draw upon an example using measurement of brain waves. In our normal conscious state, the brain produces beta waves, from 18 to 40 cycles per second. Our brain functions in this state as we go about our daily lives, walking, eating, talking, shopping, and working. Yet each of us also experiences an increase in slower brain waves, between 8 and 12 cycles per second, called alpha brain waves. This wave occurs when we feel relaxed or "centered" with feelings of well being.

The alpha state also activates creative daydreaming with eyes closed. There are other brain states as well, such as the theta state (4 to 7 cycles per second, dominant at ages 2 to 5) and the delta wave state (1 to 3 cycles per second during deep sleep). It is in the alpha wave state where healing is most effective. A person can move from the beta wave state to alpha wave state by stimulation of music or other sound that is soothing and that feels good. In this healing mode, other physiological effects occur, such as a marked decrease in the body's oxygen consumption (respiration rate), a decrease in the heartbeat on the average of three beats per minute, and a decrease in metabolic rate.

In the early 1960s researchers began studying the "split brain." In 1980 Roger Sperry, M.D., won a Nobel prize for his research in physiology and medicine. He discovered that the two cerebral hemispheres of the brain had distinct functions. The left, usually the dominant side, is involved in reasoning, language, writing, and reading. The right side, usually the less dominant side, is more involved in nonverbal processes, such as art, music, and creative behaviors. There has been an explosion of research linking specific brain processes to musical experience. Many results from these studies have been presented in conferences at prestigious medical schools and universities, and much of this information has been summarized by Arthur Harvey in a seven-part videotape series produced by Eastern Kentucky University named *Music and the Brain*. Harvey is a music educator who was on the faculty of the University of Louisville School of Medicine for five years in the Department of Psychiatry and Behavioral Sciences. He assisted in the development of the Program of Arts in Medicine. He has published many articles on music and brain research and is featured on the video series. Harvey notes many of the findings from current research including the following:[7]

- Music pitch (highness or lowness of a sound) is processed in the right hemisphere of the brain.

---

[7]By written permission of Dr. A. Harvey.

- Musical image processing is mostly in the right hemisphere of the brain.

- Music-information processing is found predominately in the left hemisphere of the brain.

- Rhythm is perceived temporally and therefore is processed in the left hemisphere of the brain.

- Melody is perceived as patterns and therefore is processed in the right hemisphere.

- Music can affect the reticular activating system and therefore can be used to control holographic memory.

- Music activates the thymus gland functioning.

- Music sets up a natural resonance between the limbic system and cerebral cortex, whose open communication is important for personality integration and individuation, as well as psychic health.

The more educational training a person has in music, the more they will listen to music with the left brain.

Soothing music seems to lower the level of catecholamines (chemicals such as adrenaline).

Because music is processed in the limbic system prior to cerebral processing, many brain-damaged and profoundly retarded individuals can respond directly to music, excluding cerebral cognition.

The diagram on the following page shows the areas of the brain where music is processed. This is the limbic system or midbrain, which is called the paleomammalian brain. This part of the brain contains memory and personal identity, and is the center of strong, controlling emotions. It includes the pituitary gland (the "master control" gland of the body), the hypothalamus (controlling visual attention, anxiety, and attention span), the olfactory cortex (smell), and the endocrine glands (hormone levels, hunger and thirst, sex drive, and sleep).

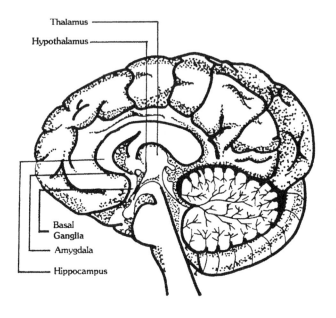

Thalamus

Hypothalamus

Basal
Ganglia

Amygdala

Hippocampus

According to the summary of research in *Music and the Brain: Studies in the Neurology of Music* there are at least three neurophysical healing processes which may be triggered by music (Critchley and Hensen 1977):

Because music is nonverbal, it can move through the brain's auditory cortex directly to the center of the brain's limbic system. From there it influences the midbrain network which governs most emotional experiences and such basic metabolic responses as body temperature, blood pressure, and heart rate.

Music may activate the flow of stored memory and imaginal material across the corpus callosum, a bridge between the left and right hemispheres of the brain, helping the two to work in harmony. Carl Jung, the imminent psychologist who advanced the now widely-accepted psychological theories of archetypes and synchronicity, felt that bringing certain emotionally charged images to awareness relieved neurotic symptoms. In other words, it made us whole. (These ideas form the foundation for the GIM process of psychotherapy with music, which will be presented in more detail in Chapter 5.)

Music is thought to excite peptides and stimulate endorphins, natural opiates secreted by the hypothalamus that produces a feeling of euphoria.

A complete series of studies on the neurological aspects of music is compiled in the Critchley and Henson book. Their book contains data essential for therapists and others who want to pursue the study of music and healing from a medical perspective.

Music's effect on the brain has been well documented and forms the foundational theory supporting the use of prescriptive sound.

PART 2

The many uses of Prescriptive Sound

Music is a fair and glorious gift of God.

MARTIN LUTHER KING, JR.

INTRODUCTION

In my quest to understand "healing music" methods, and the holistic, emotional and physiological effects of music, I have found that some of the most effective methods and philosophical approaches are those of Helen Bonny, creator of Guided Imagery and Music (GIM), and A. A. Tomatis, M.D., creator of the Tomatis Method. Each is a pioneer working in the field of music healing, and draws upon knowledge of the past, while adding contemporary insights.

I have also discovered two effective tools for complementing healing methods: the Betar instrument and the Somatron table. I will describe these unique tools in further detail in later chapters of this book. I have personally experienced and studied the Bonny and the Tomatis works and have learned how to operate the Betar instrument. I have a Somatron table and have worked with clients in private sound therapy sessions using this table.

Carl Jung, eminent pioneering psychiatrist of the twentieth century, had an interesting thing to say about music, as quoted in *Carl Jung, Wounded Healer of the Soul* (Dunne 2000, 190). "Music he listened to sparingly because, as he told pianist Margaret Tilly, 'Music is dealing with such deep archetypal material and those who play don't realize this. Yet, used therapeutically, from this level, music should be an essential part of every analysis. It expresses in sounds what fantasies and visions express in visual images. … music represents the movement, development, and transformation of motifs of the collective unconscious.'"

In the next few chapters of this book we will explore these methods in further detail and study the tools of using prescriptive sound. I will include examples from my own work and offer suggestions for the application of them.

When approaching the methods used in music healing, we should keep in mind the following questions:

What kinds of music have the greatest healing qualities? For what purposes?

What has already been documented and proved?

CHAPTER 5

The Bonny Method: Guided Imagery and Music (GIM)

Helen Bonny, Ph.D., CMT, co-founder of Guided Imagery and Music, formulated a psychotherapy model using music. She was chairperson of the Music Therapy Department in the School of Music at Catholic University of America, Washington, D.C., a position that featured her unique approach to music and psychotherapy. GIM is a music-assisted interactive therapy which facilities explorations of consciousness that can lead to transformation and wholeness.

In 1969, Bonny was a Research Fellow at Maryland Psychiatric Institute in Baltimore. Along with Dr. Stan Groff, she designed music listening programs for the patients using LSD and music. Her own transcendent experiences while playing her violin some years before had given her insight into the healing power of music. During her work at the psychiatric institute she created tapes to help accomplish the following five therapeutic objectives:

- Help patients relinquish usual controls and enter more fully into the inner world of experience, and to foster deep relaxation

- Facilitate the release of intense emotionality and blocked psychic energy

- Contribute toward peak experience and self-awareness

- Provide continuity in an experience of timelessness

- Direct and structure the experience: clarify personal values, and explore the inner self

The GIM method uses only classical music as the most appropriate structure for use with psychotherapy. Bonny felt this music had the most depth and feeling and expedited the movement of deep feelings and/or image catharsis, which is the aim of the therapy. Her selection of the music was based on intuitive knowledge, extensive classical music theory training as a music therapist and musician, many years of research at the Maryland Institute, and her work with hundreds of people in her workshops. GIM claims there are many people who benefit from the therapy, and some who cannot: schizophrenics or non-verbalizing subjects, drug abusers, and people who really dislike classical music.

Shortly after she designed these tapes, Bonny began creating the Guided Imagery and Music experiences with music. She initially used this whole method with those who were close to her. She related this story (Bonny and Savory 1973):

It was winter and a group of seven friends were snowbound in her home on a wintry morning in February 1972. Unable to attend church, she suggested they try an experiment using music and had the seven people lie on the floor to experience the music. She had designed a 45-minute tape and guided them with the imagery suggestions written by Dr. Hans Carl Leuner in 1969. The method was called Guided Affective Imagery (GAI) and it prepares the patient for evocative and therapeutic imagery.

The patient lies down on a couch. Outer stimuli are reduced as much as possible. The room should be quiet and the lights dimmed. Relaxation is suggested and verbal suggestions that help deepen the relaxation are given.

The therapist asks the patient to imagine a meadow, any meadow that comes to mind. No further comment is given. Everything is left open so the patient can develop his or her own image of a meadow with its associated feeling quality. The therapist gently persists in asking the patient to give a detailed description of his imagery and the feelings associated with it.

Originally, music was not used, but was added later by others, including William Trussel of the Menninger Clinic in Topeka, Kansas, and John Lobell of the Maryland Center. Initial choices of music for GIM were made on the basis of intuition, that is, by a kind of direct and immediate knowing without the conscious use of reasoning. These intuitions were further tested by a more approved scientific approach, through consensus with other practitioners and with clients.

Further, selections according to standard musical qualities and variables were used, including pitch (high, middle, low tones), rhythm and tempo, vocal and/or instrumental moods, melody and harmony, and timbre (color or sound a melody makes on one instrument versus another).

For each tape Bonny selected a classical composition of music. She found people responded more favorably to classical music than to any other type. It evoked greater enjoyment and interest with repeated hearings, and had a more intricate sound. Bonny felt pop, rock, and jazz directed the attention to itself as entertainment and did not facilitate personal experience. New Age music, to her, was not structured enough. She felt that people get bored with too many simplistic sounds and that after a few hearings of this music the sameness of the dynamics became irritating rather than restful. She explains:[8]

---

[8] Bonny lecture at the American Holistic Medical Association, Seattle, Washington, 1986.

No definitive studies have been made to determine which tape of music and/or selections have the greatest healing qualities. Before this can be accomplished, more information must be discovered as to the variables within music and how they specifically affect certain people. For the variables in music are diverse; people's taste in music is diverse, and habitual listening postures have an effect because one hears music differently according to the posture when listening; that is, standing, walking, sitting and lying down. When one is lying down, relaxation happens faster, and it is easier to slip into deep unconscious states. There is a greater focus, less attention to the outer body.

The GIM tapes were designed through Bonny's research at the Maryland Psychiatric Research Center. Each tape has six stages:

- Pre-onset
- Onset
- Build to a peak
- Peak
- Stabilization
- Return

I will analyze three of the GIM tapes: Comforting/Anaclytic, Beginner's Group Experience, and Affect Release.

Comforting/Anaclytic. The theme of this recording is warmth, comfort, and nurturance. The GIM therapy leads one back spontaneously to important early childhood memories with the stimulus of resonant cello sounds and male/female vocals, which evoke childhood feelings, and male/female relationships currently acting upon the individual. It is one of the longer programs (44 minutes) and contains the following selections:

- Haydn: *Cello Concerto in C,* Adagio

- Sibelius: *Swan of Tounella*

- Villa-Lobos: *Bachianas Brasileiras, No. 5*

- Boccherini: *Cello Concerto in B Flat Major,* Adagio

- Glinka: *Ivan Susanin,* Act 4, Scene 2

- Schubert: Songs from *Die Schone Mullerin,* "Der Neugierige," Second Song

- Debussy: *Girl with Flaxen Hair*

The balanced complement of vocal and instrumental selections arranged on this tape, all in a similar or associated key, help one composition flow into another and maintain continuity of feeling for the listener. The mellowness of the cello, and the lower range, along with the sustained orchestral sounds, provide a musical setting of comfort and reverie. The female and male voices in the Villa-Lobos, Glinka, and Schubert pieces frequently foster recollections of conversations.

Beginner's Group Experience. This tape was designed as a diagnostic tape for the GIM experience. Bonny used Dr. Leuner's procedure (Leuner found music sessions predictive of phenomenology which later was dealt with in detail during verbal therapy). Leuner details ten standard imagery situations, and this tape uses six:

- Relaxing in a meadow

- Exploring a house as a symbol of the person

- Following a brook upstream to its source

- Climbing a mountain and describing the view

- Following a brook downstream to the ocean

- Returning to normal consciousness

The music selections on this tape include:

- Meadow: Ravel, *Daphnis and Chloe*, Suite No.2, Part 1
- House: Brahms, *Symphony No.1,* Third Movement
- Brook Upstream: Respighi, *Pines of Rome, Gianicola*
- Mountain Top: Tschesnekoff, *Salvation Is Created*
- Brook Downstream: Debussy, *Nocturne, Les Sienes*
- The Return: Pachelbel, *Canon in D*

This tape is ideal to use with workshops and other group experiential sessions, as well as individual sessions with clients. It contains visual imagery sequences that give the patient an understanding of different areas of him/herself and prepares the patient for a more involved exploration. The last piece, Pachelbel's *Canon,* a well-known and loved piece, has rhythmic motion representing a rocking or swaying sensation, reminiscent of prenatal experience.

Affect Release. This is a special purpose tape. It is used in the workshop situation when tension and acting-out behavior is present or in individual sessions when the subject has strong feelings of grief, fear, or anger and difficulty releasing them. The music selections urge release; in fact, they have a tone of insistence. As soon as release is accomplished, the tape is removed, or changed to another one. Selections include:

- Holst: *The Planets,* "Mars"
- Bach: *Toccata and Fugue in D Minor*
- Orff: *Carmina Burana,* "Fortuna"
- Verdi: *Messa Da Requiem,* "Dies Trae"

According to Bonny, if this is played for a person in a normal state, it would probably evoke a war-like imagery, or violence, so it would not be helpful from a therapeutic view. If the subject were already angry, this tape would provide a catalyst to help them externalize the emotion. The seven-minute "Mars" piece is very effective for this. The second piece, by Bach, brings a new infusion of energy and, for some, feelings of power. The third piece is a rhythmic chorale expression. It is like a "second crack" at anger. The first three pieces are designed to affect release. A strong rhythmic context is in the music to help promote security. The listener can then go deeper into personal experience. The last piece, a quieter, vocal passage, promotes renewal and return.

How the Tapes Are Used

There are four main objectives in music program/therapy methods:

- Insights into presenting to a patient problem areas with resulting behavior change in everyday life interactions.

- Indications of greater spontaneity and adaptability (freedom) leading to self-actualization.

- An opportunity for creative problem solving, decision making, and goal planning.

- A greater interest in and appreciation of great music.

The tape selection is based on the Iso principle described in Chapter 3. That is, the therapist must be able to determine the psychological state of the subject and to select appropriate music to match the state of mind. A GIM session lasts from one and one half to two hours and is conducted in a fairly soundproofed private room, with a comfortable couch or reclining chair. Eyeshades, stereo headset and blanket are made available, and the tapes are played on a high-quality music listening machine.

A preliminary interview is given to provide information about the client's life history, and the GIM method is explained.

Next is the induction (relaxation and concentration exercise). Induction can be done in a variety of ways. One way is to ask the person to tense a muscle as tightly as possible, then to relax that same muscle. For instance, starting at the feet, the patient tenses it as much as he/she can, then relaxes the feet. The process continues from foot to calf, to thigh, and up through the rest of the body including the stomach, back, chest, and so forth.

The next step, concentration, asks the person to focus on one stimulus to the exclusion of all others. This focus or concentration can be a guided fantasy with a story theme. A story is told and when the voice ceases, appropriate music is played. During the music, the patient is urged to continue the ongoing narrative and bring the story to conclusion.

Last, the music listening period encourages the patient to verbally relate his/her impressions, fantasies and feelings as they occur in response to the music. The therapist uses the techniques of reflection, introspection, Gestalt, and empathy to deeply involve the patient in the experience. It is important to note that the therapist does not interpret the imagery during or after a session.

When the music comes to a close the therapist suggests the listener return slowly to normal consciousness and take time to recall the images and feelings he or she experienced during the experience. Care is taken to be sensitive to the slightly altered state (which carries over into the post-session period) of feeling vulnerable and open.

During a verbal integration time, the listener shares with the therapist what is easy and natural to relate. He/she is encouraged to write down during the following week any events and thoughts that may relate to the music listening session. Often the therapist recommends a series of sessions, the number to be decided upon and contracted by therapist and subject. GIM therapy is used to explore extraordinary states of consciousness and sometimes requires a number of explorations for the patient to feel completely comfortable with the experience and to benefit from its results.

Certain types of people and illness categories respond more favorably to GIM than others. The best subjects are well motivated for treatment because their belief system allows for a new and innovative approach. Being knowledgeable about music is not a necessary attribute. Also it is not necessary for a subject to elicit imagery for therapy to be beneficial. Emotional responses and kinesthetic reactions can form the basis for self-understanding. Non-imagers can follow a stream of consciousness that often leads to spontaneous retrieval of information not reached in other forms of therapy.

Types of Imagery Stimulated through Music[9]

Stream of Consciousness Imagery: Exploring surface images, superficial, a bridge to other depths, real life situations or incidences. Feel change in energy. Cannot concentrate on one thing too long. What is actually going on in present life.

Kinesthetic or Sensory Imagery: Body movement and awakening, seeing, smelling, touching; changes in state of consciousness, indications of newness, tingling, pain, tightness, numbness, parts of body opening. Can be bridge to a deeper experience, changes in body size, change in feelings, temperature changes in body, "I'm spinning," or "I'm flying," most primal imagery, preverbal, most challenging, no words.

Memory Imagery: Personal symbols, age regression, might ask "why now?" Rich imagery for personal healing experiences, fill out

[9] (McKinney 1990, 34)

imagery here in more detail. Feelings associated with memory surface, psychodynamics in correlation to current life situations develop and strengthen imagery here.

Feeling Imagery: Crying, tears, choking, coughing, sobbing, wailing, sniffling, laughing, smiling, giggling, smirking.

Archetypal Imagery: Universal, mountains, oceans, trees, shadow figures, fairytale figures, transformation, rituals, ceremonies, historical figures. Earth Mother, the Grail, mandala, Old Man, body type, personality type, your story.

Transpersonal Imagery: Growth, flight, goes beyond the personal (ego) boundaries. Moving deeper into higher self or own wisdom, may need support here. Voice may change to lower and softer tone, peak experience, religious or spiritual experience, awesome and scary.

Healing Imagery: Brings a traveler into energy, light, warmth, vibration. Pulsing, tingling, energy explosions, draining or infilling, body cues, growing or blooming, mending or sewing up of body. Expressions of peace, deep sighing, ecstasy, change in breathing, change in skin color, release of energy, release of substance from body, water, cleansing of body.

Stuck Imagery: Nothing happening, darkness, cannot see anything, cannot move, cannot get out of something, cannot feel anything.

Metaphorical Fantasy Imagery: Anything that reflects back on life through metaphor. Loss of ego boundaries. In the imaginal realm things are different than they are in our everyday waking world. The sense of time may be shortened or lengthened. You can have experiences you've only read about. You can travel differently, fly without getting hurt, travel in or out of the body, hear and speak differently.

Experiences Using GIM Therapy

One of my subjects was a man who worked as a bookkeeper/accountant. He was interested in learning how to "image." He was ill and wanted to participate in his own healing by using visualization. But he stated that he could not recall his dreams or see images in his mind. GIM activates the imaginal realm of the mind through its selection of music. During his first session I used an induction for him to imagine himself sitting on a beach. After he was relaxed and focused on the imagined scene, I invited him to "go with the music and let it take you where you need to go," and to experience the pleasant memory of being at the sea. I asked him to verbalize what he felt and saw or imagined as he experienced the music.

Tape: Beginner's Group.

Induction: Client pictures himself sitting on a beach. Client is directed to let the music take him where he needs to go.

Man's words:
"I felt a chill go through me…a soaring feelings of rising in the air. Before that I had a sensation of being outdoors. Now I feel like dancing and am surrounded by dancers. Now I am feeling like a child again (in saying it, it went away…the feeling). When I try to convey what I am feeling I lose it. I do not really get into the music because I was getting into my reaction…when I tell you something I lose it. At one point [Pachelbel] I started to feel I was somewhere where there was a big feast. I am thinking about food. Long tables with food piled high. When I don't think "thinking" I can experience it…the music. One brief spell I looked out on a blue sky…pretty soft sky, lots of clouds floating. At another time I saw a formless…(I stopped seeing it when I tried to tell you). What I really have to do is take some of the left brain (I can really feel my left

brain!!…how did I do that?) If only I could stop trying and let go…"Let me take care of this" is what I hear. The scenes I talked about I created…imagined…I "thought" about it. I did not see them. At one point I saw a face!! Almost a full face (think it was my mother). It was just a flash just out of the corner of my eye… she wore eyeglasses, gold frame over the ears. Left brain said: "What comes next? Why is my mother's face coming?"

Some people receive insights into life experiences they have thought about for a long time. A woman who wanted a deeper knowledge about music listening had the following experience:

Tape: Relationships.

Induction: Sitting on the beach.

Woman's words:
I go to a cave where I see a lot of crystals. A little nature Spirit, like "Tinkerbell" takes me into a huge room, showing me how there is music in the crystals. By focusing on different crystals you can hear a different music. Something about … everyone used to have music in their minds … now it is thought to be just something which comes over the air waves. The real music is not that way. The mind is a kind of crystal set, really. Listening to music aids in changing channels in the mind. If you can let the music do this, it gives a different perspective … new shape to your being. The tiny high notes of the music stimulates my left brain. I have a sense the harp is more between the left/right brain (a celestial quality is more right-brained). Music teaches you how to create. When you get in that mood you cannot feel without visualizing at the same time. Music puts you in the space of experiencing the essence of the thing you want to see at the time you see it in your mind. There are many places in the mind I would not ordinarily go…mysterious, unknown… my programming would say "no"…music takes me all

the way through it. The high notes "beckon" to me to keep going, following the music.

In the imaginal realm, things are different from what they are in everyday life. You have different experiences that in ordinary thinking, would not happen. Time is shortened or made longer, colors are more brilliant, and you can fly, swim, and so forth without effort. Some life situations are shown with resolution.

A recently divorced woman, feeling lonely and having unresolved feelings about her life, experienced the following:

Tape: Transitions.

Induction: Pathway in the woods. Enter house, sit in a room with large window. Let the music take you through the window.

Woman's words:
The music makes me move around…I can see everywhere … I am on a mountaintop. I feel free…I jump up and down. Now I sit on the grass. It seems as though the sky is opening. I see people… they're happy (don't know them). Another time (in the 1920s?) I see women with long dresses and men with top hats… now I see the planets…miles and miles… (still by myself)…I feel really good. I have a wand…I let the rays touch my house and everything is okay.

Back on the mountain, lying on my back, looking up at the sky. Now I am walking…through some woods. It is peaceful and I look beyond the trees. I move towards the light… the sunlight (I'm still alone). I see an old beau. He just smiles… we hug. He is leading me now…through the woods by a stream…feelings of joy… glad to see one another. He asks me if I want to go across the stream. I say yes. I take off my shoes, he does too. We go across the stream. I feel the rocks under my feet…not all that pleasant. I slip off them…but he is still there. We're near the edge and I don't know how we're going to get out of the water! We move to where it is more shallow …we can step up now. He is helping me up. We're out now. We embrace and walk along the edge now. Feels really great … I feel safe, really okay. I see people now. I speak to everyone …they speak to me and "us," like we know everyone there. We hug everyone… everyone is so beautiful. I feel great peace. He says he loves me…I am special…I do have an important work to do…the way is made." [Tears.]

In a workshop talk entitled "Immediacy: Being in the Now," presented by Bonny in 1985 at the National Conference of Art Therapies, she gave an insight into a key attribute of music listening. In looking at her own life, she realized her mind had not communicated with her body at levels deep enough to make a difference in her health challenge of heart disease.

She said she was "a product of her time, which had cut off body from mind." As she worked with music in her own challenge, she applied a very deep concentration method. During this time, she observed the same immediacy of being fully present in the concentration experience is also required in music listening, and in music performing—that is, one-pointed surrender to the music.

In the GIM therapy method, concentration on music is essential to its effectiveness. The therapist often gives verbal suggestion to the listener as he/she engages in the GIM experience: "Focus on the music … and let it take you where you need to go." This is a real key to healing with sound and music.

It is important to note that not all people are suitable for the GIM therapy. It works well with clients who are capable of symbolic thinking and can also differentiate between symbol and reality. Patients with psychosis are not suited, as the process may push them further into psychosis. Though GIM is used in one-to-one therapy situations, it is also very effective in group experiences. Members of a group stimulate intervention, for instance.

GIM has evolved through many years. There are presently more than sixty-five fully trained facilitators who have completed a three-year training. Trainings are held in many countries as well as the United States, including England, Australia, New Zealand, Sweden, Denmark, Switzerland, and Germany. There are several books and many published articles that have been written reporting expanded clinical applications and procedures. This has established the work as a viable music therapy approach.

For further information, contact:
The Bonny Foundation
(866)345-5465;
www.BonnyFoundation.org;
email: info@bonnyfoundation.org.

CHAPTER 6

The Tomatis Method:
Audio-Psycho-phonology

A second method of prescriptive music is used by Dr. A. A. Tomatis (1920–2001), a French physician and specialist in otolaryngology (ear, nose, and throat). This method focuses on a meter of auditory stimulation that retrains the ear to correct the "shutting down" of listening which is a cause of poor communication and other language-oriented developments. Tomatis believed traumatic events, occurring as early as prenatal life, may cause a "cutting off" of listening. The child may simply lose the desire and ability to use the ear. Autism, for Tomatis, is the purest form of "non-listening." Helen Keller said the loss of seeing cuts us off from the world of things, but the loss of hearing cuts us off from the world of people.

There was a young man who told me his story of what it was like to live in a world where he could not hear or communicate. He was born with a brain tumor. At the age of three years his parents made a decision to have surgery performed which would save his life. When the tumor was removed he developed learning disabilities, including dyslexia.

In early school years he was delegated to the corners of the room by the teacher, and had great difficulty learning as well as socializing with his peers. His parents bought a new stereo unit. With the stereo came a free set of recordings of baroque music. He noticed when he went into his room to study behind a closed door, the family would leave him alone. He played the baroque music and after several months began to notice he could read and study better. At another time he went into a monastery where he participated in Gregorian chant. He noticed his ability to hear and communicate improved. Today he has a doctorate in psychology and is helping many others with the same difficulty he had in learning and hearing.

The Tomatis Method is based on a physiological and neurological model, with focus on the brain and early development of the ear. It addresses underlying physiological and psychological issues in a different way than GIM. The Tomatis Method uses music to develop listening and language, rather than strictly psychological processing. Both are healing modes and aim to retrieve the source of psychological blocks.

The Electronic Ear

Through sound, the Tomatis Method stimulates the main phases of a child's listening and communication development. An electronic device called the Electronic Ear modifies the sounds of music or voice. This machine, a stereo system connected with a set of headphones, a microphone, and certain filters, provides a working model of the human ear (see diagram below). The purpose of this device is to open the ear to listening by exercising the middle ear muscles. It tunes the ear in frequency ranges which may be closed. In other words, it helps one to hear more.

The Electronic Ear demonstrates that you have to be able to "hear" a sound before you can receive its greatest benefit, just as you have to be able to "hear" another person before you can really communicate. In Tomatis's research, he clearly identifies a link between

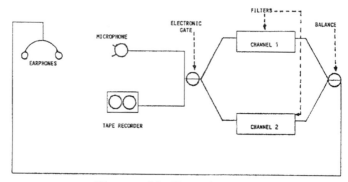

Diagram of the Electronic Ear.

problems in listening and severe disorders of the psyche. Not being able to listen has devastating effects on personal development and adjustment in an individual's life. The process of re-educating the ear to hear includes using high frequency sounds and modeling corrected language skills. According to Tomatis, the re-education process can also simultaneously clear up unconscious material.

Tomatis was the first to appreciate the important neurophysiological distinction between hearing and listening. He believed ear and auditory processes in language development are very important. As we hear and understand the sounds of language years before we learn to speak and write, we imitate the spoken language of song, nursery rhymes, and sounds. Every sound we hear is recorded in the brain. Hearing may be normal but that does not mean that we listen effectively. For example, Tomatis says: "Hearing is a passive process in which sound is simply perceived."

Listening is an active, focusing process, which allows for a precise analysis of sounds to be heard. The listening function is closely related to attention span, vigilance, and concentration. It plays a major role in integration, understanding, and retention of sound messages, especially language sounds, and is vitally important in the learning process. The better you hear, the more motivated you are to learn. Do you feel you receive from the world enough of the sounds you hear? Do you feel your life is rich with sound, or is it flat sometimes?

Tomatis's definition of "listening ability" includes both a motivational and a neurophysiological component. Real dialogue with another also means listening. Most people simply make monologues; they listen less than they talk. That is not language, but is a kind of hidden autism. Listening is essential for dialogue and is necessary for the formation of your own thought. If the cortex of the brain is not awakened properly by real listening and sound making (as it can be in early childhood), thinking cannot elaborate itself in the brain.

Reaching far back to the source of our hearing, in the womb, Tomatis found the filtered sound we hear of the mother's voice and other sounds from her are all high frequency. The fetus is literally nourished by these sounds. Listening to filtered music through the Electronic Ear retrains the muscles of the middle ear to accommodate or attune to the higher harmonics of any sound source. The pattern of uterine dialogue which should have started the process of listening may not have been established. With the Tomatis Method it can be recreated. This method is a means of retrieving the open listening which is our birthright.

Tomatis's early research with professional singers led him to conclude another aspect of listening regarding frequency levels. The individual's own voice contains only what his/her ear can hear. The fluency or ease with which the individual expresses him/herself is also part of the self-listening process. In other words, a great singer such as the famous Enrico Caruso (who actually came to Dr. Tomatis when his voice began losing its tone and was helped by Tomatis to extend the beauty of his voice) had a beautiful full range voice not only because of his large chest cavity or large mouth cavity, as some might assume, but because his ear could hear many harmonics and high frequencies.

As we develop, listening ability can be affected by physical and/or psychological factors. The following is a list of symptoms commonly observed in individuals who have learning and communication problems (Tomatis 1988):

- Need to have instructions repeated.

- Restlessness, distractibility, daydreaming, poor attention in learning communication situations.

- Tendency to misinterpret what is being said, which produces off-reaction and impedes communication with others.

- Difficult to follow or participate in conversations in noisy environments.

- Slow, hesitant, poorly articulated speech.

- Voice that is too soft or too loud.

- Difficulty sustaining interest of a group while making a speech or presentation.

- Clumsiness or awkwardness in body movement. Poor balance.

- Poor organization and planning skills.

- Poor spatial orientation and sense of time.

- Lack of curiosity or interest in learning.

- Tendency to withdraw or avoid communication in social situations.

The following are some events that have a high incidence among individuals who have the symptoms just sited:

- Difficult circumstances surrounding pregnancy.

- Under-achievement in school or on the job.

- Delay in language development, and motor development.

- Recurring ear infections in first years of life.

- Slow or poorly established preference for right/left hand.

- Difficult birth or early separation from mother as a result of illness or adoption.

Tomatis's Three Fundamental Laws

The voice reproduces only what the ear can hear.

When hearing is corrected and the missing frequencies restored, these frequencies are automatically restored to the voice, too.

Hearing which is compulsory, continual, and repeated over a period of time, modifies hearing and speech.

When the Tomatis Method of sound therapy is used, these are the cumulative results. These results have been documented over a period of thirty years:

- Easier, more efficient sleep, with shortened sleep time from two to three hours.

- New vitality and sense of well-being.

- Deep relaxation.

- Curing of disorders stemming from imbalance of inner ear fluid: nausea dizziness, tinnitus.

- Alleviation of stammering and other speech defects.

- Help for dyslexia, hyperactivity, behavioral problems in children.

- Weight loss. Slowing of metabolism and easing of stress acts as a natural appetite suppressant.

- Heightened creativity and mental capacity. Improved memory, concentration and learning abilities.

Selection of Music

Specially selected music is used in the Electronic Ear to retrain the listener. Music is a highly organized series of sounds that the ear has to analyze. Therefore, listening to music is an excellent way for anyone to learn how to perceive sounds in an organized fashion.

The main characteristics of music (tonal pitch, timbre, intensity, and rhythm) are all found in spoken language. For this reason, music prepares the ear, voice, and body to listen to, integrate, and produce language sounds. Music can be considered a pre-linguistic language since it has all the characteristics of speech except semantic value. Three kinds of music information normally used during the listening program include Mozart's music, Gregorian chant, and children's songs.

Paul Madaule writes in his article "Music and the Tomatis Method,"

> In observing the effects of different kinds of music, Tomatis came to the conclusion that few of them produced the sought after therapeutic effects on the listening function. For instance, "Chopin-type" of music has a relaxing effect but in some cases may reinforce daydreaming and absent-mindedness, tendencies which are often found in children with problems in school.

Other kinds of music, such as Paganini, Wagner or military marches have an energizing effect, which may increase hyperactive and aggressive tendencies, as well as irritability in certain children.

These are also characteristics we recognized in children who have problems adapting in school. The highly rhythmic, low frequency sound of Rock, Disco and other modern music has the same effect as marching music on young people. It appeals to them because it heightens the level of body sensation but the quality of the sound diminishes the ear's ability to listen. Mozart's scores seem to achieve the most perfect balance between the relaxing and energizing effects of sound.

Most of the music used in the listening program features violin, as in Mozart's symphonies, divertimento, serenades, and concertos. This music is modified by electronic filters which remove or soften the low-pitched frequencies so as to stimulate the perception zone of the high harmonics, a zone of prime importance in the listening function.

Maria DeRungs McKinney, DMA, Director, Casa de Maria Research Center in Everett, Washington, also speaks strongly about the music of Mozart. She says all of his compositions are powerful and beneficial, and the energy patterns of his music bring strength to the physical, mental, and spiritual.

Children's songs and nursery rhymes harmonize body movements and motor functions by their effect on the vestibular system of the ear. They increase awareness of the body, and help shape the child's body image, according to proponents of the Tomatis Method. Children's songs are an excellent model of how a child approaches language. They emphasize the sound and the construction of words which have to "sound" pleasant. These songs are stimulating to hear, learn, and vocalize and act as a catalyst in the transition from the non-verbal world to the adult world of verbal communication.

The Tomatis Method does not use a wide variety of classical music. It utilizes "sounds that charge" (Mozart, Gregorian chant, and children's songs) because they have the high frequencies. Gregorian chant does not have tempo, but has rhythm, which leads the listener into tranquility. The addition of the mother's voice (if available) has a psychologically therapeutic effect.

Gregorian chant is a music which has a rhythm consistent with the breathing and heartbeat of a calm, relaxed person. Gregorian chant is a body of chant codified by Pope Gregory (590–604) in an effort to standardize the Catholic mass. It differs from music in a number of ways. It has no meter (pattern of fixed beats). Timing is not based on a rhythm noted on music sheets, but on the human breath. (The chant master who trained novices and led the chant controlled the group's respiration rate by having them sing long phrases.)

It is this extension of controlled exhalation that maintains a good tone. It slows down the breathing rate and thus slows the heartbeat. A reduction of blood pressure naturally follows. Traditional Gregorian chant by monks is done eight times daily and is a form of respiratory yoga. Physical and emotional stress is eliminated, and a profound feeling of peace fills the being. Gregorian chant is rich in timorous overtones of frequencies ranging from 2000 to 4000hz. So monks produce and listen to high frequency sounds eight hours a day. Chant is also an exercise in listening. Monks listen actively, as they chant to God, who speaks to them through their hearts.

It is interesting to note that over the past three decades, many Catholic monasteries have closed, unable to sustain operations. Tomatis claims these monasteries were not practicing Gregorian chant. A reasonable hypothesis is that cortical charge and its consequent boon to energy levels, concentration, alertness, and general well being in the monks, is an important factor in the Catholic church. Cortical charge is one of the most exciting theories of Tomatis.

Experience shows that some sounds put us to sleep (lullabies for example), some sounds keep us awake (street noises, traffic sounds), some calm us down (ocean surf, rain falling, birds singing), and some make us want to dance (rhythmic sounds). We are constantly bathed by sound, and Tomatis has spent thirty years analyzing the effects of sound on the physiology. The claim that music exerts a profound effect on us is an understatement.

In a lecture given in Paris in 1978, Tomatis describes cortical charge:

> The ear is primarily an apparatus intended to provide a cortical charge in terms of electrical potential. In fact, sound is transformed into nervous influx by the ciliform cells of the cochlear vestibular apparatus. The charge of energy obtained from the influx of nervous impulses reaches the cortex, which then distributes it through out the body, toning the whole system and imparting greater dynamism to the human being.

Tomatis points out all sounds cannot effect this process of charging. High frequency sounds supply a more concentrated nervous influx than low frequency sounds (our world is bombarded with low frequency sounds of the traffic, machines, computers, refrigerators). These low frequency sounds supply insufficient energy to the cortex which eventually causes exhaustion.

The aim of the Tomatis Method is to provoke, with sonic training made up of high frequency sounds, a listening posture which causes cortical charge to energize the individual. Subjects have greater motivation and competence in work, lower susceptibility to fatigue, awareness of "dynamism," better possibilities of attention and concentration, and improved memory. The therapy is effective for both children and adults.

There are two phases of treatment on the Electronic Ear:

Passive Phase:

First is a gradual introduction to filtered sound. The music of Mozart is played (as explained before, the most successful musical themes are those rich in treble frequencies and rhythmically similar to Mozart or Gregorian chant). The lower frequencies are slowly removed. For children (and for adults where it is needed) the mother's voice is not recognizable until the end of the passive phase when low frequencies reintroduced. In this phase, the filtered high frequency sounds generate neural energy, creating a "charging" effect which stimulates the cortex and cortical functions including communication. During the sessions, the children are free to draw, paint, or play with others in a specially designed room. Adolescents and adults have their own area where they can take their prescribed sessions. When certain behavioral signposts and test results appear, the second part can begin. These are:

- More tolerance, less frustration
- Better comprehension (listens more, talks more)
- Self-confidence (tries harder)
- Interest in reading
- Mental alertness, higher level of energy
- Greater involvement with everyday life
- Test results of higher frequency hearing.

Second, is gradual defiltration of filtered music. This phase simulates the transition from a liquid prenatal acoustic environment to the postnatal acoustic environment. This is called the sonic birth. (The sonic birth phase is the after-birth phase, when, in the first ten days of life the baby's body reabsorbs amniotic fluid in the inner ear canal.)

Active Phase:

This phase introduces language. The first stage is prelinguistic. The individual is asked to hum or sing and, in effect, prepare the voice for more structured spoken language. (Nursery rhymes or children's songs introduce children to this stage of the program.)

Next, the linguistic stage includes the presentation of more spoken language. The individual is asked to repeat words, phrases, and sentences and read aloud. Microphones transmit the voice through the Electronic Ear before being fed back to the ear through earphones and the bone conduction device. The feedback from the voice is modified to enhance the higher frequencies of higher harmonics of the voice. At the same time, increased stimulation is given to the right ear to enhance its role as leader or director in the control of the individual's own speech. Tomatis suggests that the right ear controls and analyzes sounds and has to be the heading or dominant ear to stimulate. To prepare the right ear to become the leading one, the intensity of sound fed via headphones to the left ear is progressively reduced (Tomatis, 1972).

The Tomatis Method has been successfully applied by special education teachers and psychologists in Canada, speech and language pathologists in the United States, physicians, musicians, teachers, and orthophonists in Europe, and professors in music and psychology in South Africa. These specialists received training in this method under the direction of Dr. Tomatis at the Tomatis Center in Paris, France, and continue to work in association with the center. Symptoms such as autism, dyslexia, hyperactivity, insomnia, tinnitus, and emotional disturbance have been cured. Peak performance skills for athletes and others have been achieved. There are Listening Centers in the U.S., Canada, Europe, and Latin America.[10]

---

[10]For locations see www.Tomatis.com.

Methods: A Summary

The Bonny Guided Imagery and Music system (GIM) and the Tomatis Method both use music healing models. Both models of music selection have been scientifically researched and well thought out. Both are used for children and adults, although GIM is mostly for adults. They have proven to be effective modes of healing and personal transformation. They focus on frequency wave stimulation of mind and body, and are unique in their potential to aid in music healing research.

While GIM seeks to locate memory patterns, the Tomatis Method seeks to access the prenatal experience of hearing first formed in the womb. Music therapy can be a powerful tool, but it often presumes everyone possesses a clear listening channel. Tomatis says this listening aspect is a very important clue to our psychology. Madaule says it comes as a surprise to many music therapists when the most sublime of symphonies, the most inviting of singing games, makes no impression whatsoever on some listeners.

Tomatis was the first to appreciate the important neurophysiological distinction between hearing and listening. The process of re-educating the ear to hear, using high frequency sounds and modeling corrected language skills can clear up unconscious material simultaneously, according to Tomatis.

In both these healing models using music, it is essential that the listener surrender to the flow of the music, letting it resonate throughout the whole body. Spontaneous expressions, crying, laughing, shaking, and so forth, which may be activated by the music, should be allowed to come out. It is also important to suspend intellectual thought about the music, trying to guess who the composer is, what culture it comes from, the performance quality of the orchestra, and technicalities such as what key the music is being played in. Sustained focused introspection is needed. This happens naturally if the music selection is right for the listener. It is not so much what the listener likes or dislikes but what resonates (evokes an emotional response) that determines the right music to use.

CHAPTER 7

The Betar Instrument

*It happens very rarely, but when it happens
it's worth waiting for, that the instrument
becomes part of your body.*

JACK BRYMER

Future technology is brought to us through the pioneering efforts of Peter Kelly of Lakemont, Georgia, who created a large instrument that produces state-of-the-art sound quality for music listening in his laboratory. In a white dome-shaped research laboratory (Dimensional Sciences, Inc.) is a room for the Betar (Bioenergetic-Transducer-Resonance) instrument. Peter learned about the work of music therapists, studied the effects of human energy with the energy of the environment, worked with Justin O'Brien, Ph.D., a stress reduction expert, and studied the meditative state. His laboratory contains a vast library of books on medicine, science, holism, spirituality, radionics, and more. For three years he refined the Betar into an instrument with the ability to reproduce accurately the full sonic spectrum of music.

The Betar is a psychoacoustic instrument utilizing music. No special operating methods are given. The subject experiencing it can receive the benefits by "riding the Betar." This includes stress release and in-depth imaging processes aided by music, which allows unconscious materials that have become blocked to come to the surface of the mind.

Both of these potent instruments, the Betar and Somatron, were created by persons who had no background in music, nor understanding of the many variables in music but were simply interested in creating an instrument that would produce the closest possible facsimile to pure sound.

The research on the Betar was gathered by the experience of some 2,000 people who have ridden the Betar in the laboratory, and it was shown that it can indeed be a healing instrument. It is a geodesic structure in the shape of a duodecahedron frame, which looks like a giant jungle gym. A padded table or bed, swinging free from chains attached to the frame, floats in the center. In front of this is a panel of stereophonic state-of-the-art equipment with shelves full of compact laser disc music recordings. An operator at the panel orchestrates the experience.

The rider lies on the padded bed at the center of the Betar structure. As the lights are turned down the music is turned on. The Betar has a high quality amplifier capable of accurately producing a clear (near direct current) continuous flow of 50,000 cycles per second radio wave range sound. Bedini, Carver, and Technics make the amplifiers. Eight speakers are arranged in a special way to set up a holographic bubble of sound, with very little distortion.

The geodesic structure is open but its form gives the impression of containment. Psychologists say this is good design, as it allows support without a person's becoming claustrophobic from being in an enclosure. Music is played at an average of 80 decibels, loud but not dangerously so. (In terms of loudness, which is measured in units called decibels, sound can be harmful. The effects of loud sounds as contributors of hearing loss have been known for years.) The following chart will give an indication of the sound intensity levels of various sounds.[11]

120 db	Threshold of pain
115 db	Ship engine room
110 db	Low-flying jet aircraft
100 db	Riveter/subway train
95 db	Motorcycle
85 db	Heavy traffic
75 db	Vacuum cleaner
70 db	Normal conversation
60 db	Department store/normal conversation
50 db	Average office/living room
40 db	Quiet office/library
30 db	Quiet day in country/softest orchestra
20 db	Whisper
10 db	Gentle breeze
0 db	Threshold of hearing

Even though the amplitude of sound on the Betar is louder than one would usually listen to, one hardly notices this after listening for a brief time. Because the quality of the music is so refined, it seems one becomes a part of the music. In principle, the Betar creates an energy envelope, which interacts with the energy of the subject. If the subject is out of balance, this energy will tend to affect the output of the Betar, often causing a change in the quality of the sound being played. By adjusting the specific frequencies of the sound

---

[11] Chart created by Justin O'Brien.

Experiencing the Betar.

spectrum with the graphic equalizer, the Betar and the rider are brought into balance.

There are three important aspects of the Betar which make it powerful:

Phase Conjugation:

A unique phenomenon normally associated with laser physics, involves a plumbing of longitudinal sound waves below 200 hertz (cycles per second, the rate at which sound vibrates). This allows small amounts of energy as information to be added as subliminals during the music experience without distracting from the music program. These subliminals include the hertz frequencies associated with the seven main energy centers of the body.[12]

CHAKRA	NUMBER OF HERTZ
Base	4
Sacral	6
Solar	10

---

[12] This chart was given to me by Peter Kelly in 1988.

Heart	12
Throat	16
Brow	96
Crown	96–960

This, combined with the music, allows a person's body to absorb the music and the sound waves on a very deep level. Traditional sound equipment is normally placed in a conjugation which has a pushing and pulling effect. Phase conjugation employed by the Betar is either pushing all the way or pulling all the way (the direction of the energy). This allows for a much more profound effect than normal sound.

What this means for the listener, and makes the Betar sound experience so unique, is that because of this phase conjugation, the longitudinal sound waves are not directional. Therefore they permeate the entire area. Sound does not seem to come from the speakers, but literally envelopes the listener. Kelly says the Betar is the only music instrument he knows that uses phase conjugation in sound waves, so, technologically speaking, it is unique. It sets up a parading, a holographic sound space; sound waves in real time.

Subliminals:

Subliminals are words or sounds added to music below the normal hearing threshold. Kelly says sound subliminals are more potent than spoken subliminals. Spoken mantras have been electronically broken down and replaced as sound frequencies. They are played below the amplitude of the music, and pulse along with it. They are digital tapes tested for compatibility with the system. Also, sound frequencies of 7.83 hertz (research at the time of his original research proved this to be earth's resonance frequency given off in the cavity between the stratosphere and earth's surface) are added to the subliminals. When a person hears this frequency, they again experience tranquility as if walking barefoot on an isolated beach or through the woods on a quiet day, even though you may be living in a city environment of high electromagnetic waves with all the television and radio waves around, cutting one off from the earth's resonance.

Purity of Sound:

Superior speakers, superior sound equipment, soundproofed room, and darkened environment while playing compact laser discs, make the Betar a very powerful sound experience.

The Betar instrument aids in the release of stress energies in mind and body. These released energies are directed into the ground through wiring (this has been tested through scientific methods to determine the direction of energy coming from the body) so that the room does not hold the excess.

The listening experiences are not directed. That is, the listener is not asked to do anything but lie down and relax and enjoy the music. The listener selects, and is invited to select music he particularly relates to. This determines what the facilitator mostly plays. The inventor, Peter Kelly, makes no specific results or claims relative to the experience of riding the Betar. What seems to happen is a release of tension, with corresponding benefits to the listener.

Music for the Betar is selected for the most part according to the subject's own taste and thus encompasses a wide variety of music. Unlike the Tomatis Method of selection for the Electronic Ear, the high frequency of the music does not sound and is not a factor in selection, nor do GIM criteria of using classical music apply. Music is selected according to the therapist's evaluation and request of the subject's need. For the prime intent of the Somatron design to facilitate the kinesthetic sense, music with some low (but not predominate) bass tones is needed.

A survey of over 2,000 people who have ridden the Betar shows that most of the experiences have had a healing affect, clearing the mind and helping the body release pain and stiffness. Persons who have "blocks" in creativity have benefited by being able to move past, emotionally, not being able to write, and similar problems. A Reichian therapist who came to experience the instrument said: "Riding the Betar is equivalent to two years of therapy."

A cycle of release occurs: stimulation of emotions helps release the physical body, and stimulation of the physical body (as in strong rhythms, drum, bass tones) helps release emotions. A deep resonance occurs at the cellular level. The synchronization of body rhythms and subtle feelings facilitates transcendence of ordinary consensual perception of reality, and promotes entry into visionary, non-ordinary states of consciousness. One person described her experience after a session:

> I have heard music but this is the first time I have really experienced it. I was touched to the core. It was an unobtrusive experience and I was able to go deep into my own experience and feel nurtured and supported by the music.
>
> The music was very relaxing and I found my thoughts drifting. Unlike the normal passing into the sleep state, I had a fairly extended period of clarity which was detached from the usual consciousness of body, place, and time, similar to a meditative experience. I felt like I was inside the music and that it was being projected out from me in all directions.

Although many different types of music can be played through the Betar, instrumental and New Age music is the most popular selection. The only sounds not used are heavy metal and acid rock, due to the distortions in sound. Rhythmic sounds are usually played first, to match the normal state with which the listener begins the experience. Quieter music is then played as relaxation occurs and a deeper brain state is achieved.

The duration of a typical listening session is from forty-five minutes to one hour. At least thirty minutes is recommended to allow the listener time to feel deep relaxation. The operator monitors and interacts with the listener and makes and cues selections, mixes these sources with the subliminals and controls amplitude levels. Each session is then documented for research aims.

Unusual inner experiences occur while listening to music on the Betar. The pure sound quality enables one to have a direct experience with sound, as this woman attests:

> I felt as though my body was formless energy waves interacting with and being washed through by the music. The music itself seemed to be wave forms that moved through my energy field. If I resisted the flow of the waves of the music at all on any level, it was as if my formless state changed to form until I released whatever I was holding and then the form dissolved to formlessness once again. In between notes the silence was like a move into pure consciousness between thoughts.

Another woman listened to vocal music which had a lot of meaning for her:

> Many extremes of emotions came up all the way from love, sadness, laughter, and anger. I understood for the first time what the song *Making Love Out of Nothing At All* meant to me. That song always has haunted me and I never understood why until I experienced it on the Betar. I believe I have experienced a shift in what I will and will not "go for" in my life. During the song *I Can't Go for That*, I felt renewal, strength, and courage to face whatever lies before me.

A definite kinesthetic experience such as the following occurs for almost everyone in this experience, in addition to wonderful body relaxation:

> ... A deeper breathing, relaxation, and warmth in my fore-
> head, spreading down my neck and shoulders ... a loosening
> in my rib cage ... releasing muscular tension in my abdomen
> and chest ...

Although the Betar is currently being used for stress reduction in sports centers, chiropractors' offices and hotels, many other possibilities exist for its usefulness in areas such as therapeutic counseling, pain control, teaching visualization, healing, rehabilitation, transition work (decision making), and activating psychic sensitivity. It could be placed in drug/alcohol centers, psychiatric hospitals, and prisons.

Because of the holographic sound quality of the Betar, it is the best instrument for all-around experience. It works the fastest, moves the person's emotional releases the most effectively, and utilizes the listener's own inner healing to the fullest. The sound experience has an uncanny capacity to produce synthesia, corresponding perceptions in other sensory areas to a high degree. For example, the sound of wind blowing in a piece of music may make one feel water.

The Betar requires the greatest precautions when in use. A prospective listener needs to let the Betar operator know if any of the following conditions exist:

- They have a history of seizure, heart problems, or heart
  transplant device

- They are pregnant

- They have a serious disease such as cancer, cerebral palsy,
  or MS

- They wear a hearing aid

- There is a resource support person to help them integrate afterward.

- It is difficult to determine if they are grounded in consensus reality. It is desired to have clear enough boundaries between the inner process and the external world to integrate their experience.

Holographic principles have great relevance for many areas of science and humanity. It can bring a whole new insight into understanding physiology, psychiatry, psychotherapy, and psychology. There are great possibilities and implications for spiritual, philosophical, and practical applications for healing.[13]

Experiencing the Betar many times I feel opened my sense of hearing music, increased my ability to appreciate all sounds, and accentuated the desire to learn from them all. I have really developed a new respect for the variety and richness that new technology has brought us in the sound experience. A blend of the natural and the scientific gives a whole picture of our world of sound.

---

[13] For further information, contact Dimensional Sciences at (800) 332-3827.

CHAPTER 8

The Somatron
Sound Therapy Table

Somatron is from the Greek *soma* meaning body and *tron* meaning instrument. It is an elegant body table with specially placed sound speakers inside the body of the table that produce sound and a vibro-tactile experience. It plays standard cassettes or digital compact discs, and the quality of the music is a total blending of harmonies, tones, and rhythms that touch the body at a cellular level.

The table is the creation of Byron Eakin of Tampa, Florida. The design appeared to Eakin when he was meditating. He consulted experts in the field, including physiotherapists, acoustical engineers, New Age musicians, and sound researchers. This unique application of sound energy is now protected by a U.S. patent.

All known vibrating sound instruments transmit one specific frequency or speed of vibration at a time. The Somatron transmits hundreds of different vibrating frequencies to match the music simultaneously as it converts sound into high-density vibration. The experience of lying on it with music playing provides for deep relaxation.

Through entrainment to the music, the body and brain are synchronized with the rhythms. This induces a profound state of relaxation, which occurs rapidly and spontaneously.

The Somatron is a multi-purpose table, used as both a personal and professional instrument. Professional users include physicians, music therapists, nurses, and sports teams. It is being used and researched in clinics, hospitals, holistic health centers, rehabilitation centers, nursing homes, fitness centers, beauty salons, locker rooms, and wherever there is a need for a drugless method of reducing muscular tension and stress. Pain control, high level wellness, and immune system stimulation are benefits of this form of sound therapy and can be accomplished at home. The person can lie on it after a difficult day to relieve muscle soreness, calm themselves at bedtime, and induce meditative and creative mind states, enhance learning, and practice self-hypnosis. People have often wanted to feel the vibration of music. Some have tried to create this by placing small cassette players on their stomach or put their feet against stereo speakers. Many people attend rock concerts where the volume can be dangerously high. None of these methods is entirely satisfying and none allows the direct physical contact provided by the Somatron.

Kinetic vibration is carried deep within muscular tissue for ultimate relaxation and increased metabolic vitality. Sonic vibration is specifically directed to skeletal muscles along the neck, shoulders, spine, back, thighs, and legs. The intensity of the stimulus can be adjusted in several ways. You can adjust the volume to control the overall density of sound. You can also adjust specific frequencies on the multi-band equalizer. This allows for experiencing a given vibratory frequency. Music selections stimulate profoundly moving experiences or a more relaxed, soothing feeling.

Specifically, health benefits of the use of the Somatron are numerous:

- Physiotherapists and chiropractors say there is a pumping action within the intervertebral discs, which separate the vertebrae of the spinal column. This action nourishes the discs, helping them maintain a heavy thickness, which helps keep the spine flexible.

- Fluid filled articular capsules in the spinal vertebrae are accelerated in action as they swim around the surfaces of the spine. These provide lubrication and nourishment for the vertebrae and carry away waste products. If these wastes accumulate, there is wear and tear on the joints and inflammation of the spinal column.

- Vibration is thought to stimulate movement of tissue fluids, nourishing ligaments of the spine and improving elasticity.

- Neurologically, the brain receives information about stress from the nervous system. When certain vibrations are felt, the neurotendonous spindles reduce the amount of information relayed and this in turn reduces the contractive command being sent to muscles and tendons, resulting in muscular relaxation.

Selection of music for the Somatron table should be chosen for the Somatron's propensity to magnify deep sound. That is, it is difficult to assume a piece of music will work on it unless one has actually tried it out on the table. For example, listening to a recording which has a strong low bass beat all the way through will be accented on the Somatron. The equalizer (a mechanism which can adjust the sound from low to high tones) can also be set to regulate this sound.

However, some pieces of music have overwhelmingly low tones which can be too much and hold the focus of energy in a subject's body in the low body area, the stomach and below, making it difficult to move past it, energetically. As a result, some people experience irritation or boredom. Unless one has a special purpose in mind for using the strong bass tones for "shaking loose" blocked areas in the intestinal region or a congested spinal region (which is effectively stimulated with this tone), care should be taken to find a more balanced spectrum of sound. Music can be an annoyance if not carefully chosen.

Music sessions should be personalized for the given time, place, and person. There are numerous variables to consider when a person comes for a Somatron session:

- **Physiology:** Is the person stressed, sad, tired? Can they relax?

- **Receptivity to the music:** A willingness to "surrender" to the music without expectations. People who are ill are prone to right hemispheric functioning (receptive, no judgments) and are more easily able go into imagery. Others hold onto themselves and are not able to get the full benefits from the music. However, for the most part, people are able to move past their emotions while lying on the Somatron much faster than they do just listening to the music while sitting in a chair or walking around.

- **Rapport with the facilitator:** Music alone is often not adequate to quiet the mind and body. Relaxation and trust in the facilitator are grounding, thus the person feels supported and free to let go to the experience of the music.

- **Uniqueness of the individual:** We all hear differently, according to how we patterned our hearing as children. Most people's hearing memory is remarkably strong. We must be in touch with a person's personal taste in music.

- **How well a person hears:** Hearing is a kinetic sense first. Sometimes a person has closed off their sense of feeling and hearing so they need music with more of an intensity. In his work with the Electronic Ear, Dr Tomatis discovered the loss of hearing high frequency sounds is due to psychological factors of not wanting to hear things when they were painful, as a child and even as a fetus in the womb.

• **Time of day:** For more subtle uses of music, there are different tones for morning, midday and evening which may make a great difference to the listener. Some people experienced more alertness in the morning than in the evening, for instance. Some have a metabolic system that takes longer to digest a meal, and they may be lethargic after the noon hour lunch. The discoveries taught by Eastern Indian master musicians show that certain ragas or modes played at certain times of the day or night have an alchemical effect on the vibrations of those who are experiencing it. This is probably true for other kinds of music as well.

• **Personal music preferences:** Allowing a person to choose their own music tapes may or may not be applicable to therapeutic treatment on the Somatron. For instance, an elderly person can select their favorite music. The quality of life is increased when the old favorites are played for them, and they can lie comfortably on the table with a light covering over them to stay warm. In hospice work, personal music is important to hear "one more time around," though music of a very gentle nature is important so that illness is not stirred up in the body.

Those not functioning well in the world—drug or alcohol abusers, for example—have been known to choose music which reinforces old psychological patterns. This could create a "stuck" situation in growth. One of the Somatron owners I have spoken with prefers to use music not known by the subject, something they do not listen to all the time. Hearing a different sound can make one listen more acutely and increase awareness. Mentally retarded subjects are not capable of making their own selections, generally. The following story illustrates this.

> A young man who lived at home had been mentally retarded from birth. One day he began having outbursts of violence, which he had never had before. He was taken to a hypnotherapist who helped reveal that he had been listening to his tape recorder every morning, with his favorite vocalist and guitar music. He said he became uncontrollably angry but still listened to it daily. When I listened to this tape I found discordant sounds of steel guitar with metallic grating noises. His parents had no idea that the recording could contribute to his drastic change in behavior. Prolonged exposure to the irritating sounds created real problems in his brain.

Here is an example of an experience with the Somatron: A friend of mine came over late one evening. He was in stress due to his work schedule. He could not even sit down to talk with me, but paced the floor with a Coke in his hand. I gave him a glass of spring water and had him remove his shoes and socks and lie on the Somatron table after he drank the glass of water. I put on a music recording called *One with the Eagle*, by Jim Oliver, and turned the switch on. This tape had a nice selection of fast and slow pieces on it and is in a major key. He took some deep breaths. I did a few minutes of therapeutic touch over his body, then began gentle foot reflexology. Within about twenty minutes his breathing slowed, and he went into deep relaxation. After thirty minutes he was ready to get up. He reported that his mind felt clear again, he was relaxed, and left for home to go to bed for the night.

I find the most relaxing method is simply to put the music at a low volume. It does not take long to de-stress a person and it is especially good late at night to help with a good night's sleep.

The Research

At the All Children's Hospital in St. Petersburg, Florida, the Somatron table is used in the Pediatric Oncology ward for all kinds of treatments. Everything from IVs, lumbar punctures to biopsies is performed right on the table, and the children are encouraged to bring their own music tapes as well. The hospital keeps a wide selection of tapes, such as religious music, lullabies, soothing imagery, and children's songs. The recording of Peter Alsop's *Wha'd Ya Wanna Do?* with children's laughter and voices is especially popular. The children like to hear "funny sounds" like computer-generated noises and heartbeats. This sound moves their attention away from what is going on in their treatments.

As one nurse put it, "It's the only pleasurable experience that children have to look forward to when they come to the clinic for treatment." The children's facial expressions change when they are able to relax. Some children must have morphine or Ativan in conjunction with the music.

At the Edison Developmental Center in Bay City, Michigan, the Somatron is being used as part of the treatment program for multiple-handicapped children. Three groups of patients were in the research program using the Somatron. One group had RATT syndrome, a continual wringing of the hands. The gently relaxing music of David Sun's *Sunrise* was used for these patients.

Another group is brain-damaged, with severe sensory deprivation. They experience music with more rhythm, such as *Deep Breakfast* by Ray Lynch, or *Imagination* by Inti Illimani.

The third group was learning how to operate switches, typewriters, and computers and work easier while listening to active music. By turning on the Somatron switch themselves they instantly feel the vibrations throughout their bodies, and begin to see the

The Somatron Apollo

relationship between what they do and the result of their behavior.

A note of interest: NASA-funded scientists suggest that astronauts might prevent bone loss by standing on a lightly vibrating plate for ten to twenty minutes a day. The bones and muscles of astronauts, free from the familiar strains of gravity, can weaken alarmingly. Muscles atrophy relatively quickly, while bones lose mass during prolonged exposures to weightlessness. Exercises in space using devices that mimic body weight and exert stress on the musculoskeletal system have not yet succeeded in eliminating the muscle and bone loss.

The same therapy of lying on or standing on a vibrating surface, they say, might eventually be used to treat some of the millions of people who suffer from the bone loss disease called osteoporosis. Although the vibrations are subtle they have had a profound effect on bone loss in laboratory animals such as turkeys, sheep, and rats.

Music on the Somatron

People who are seriously studying the effects of different music selections are making designed tapes for the Somatron. An acupuncture clinic in Washington, D.C. has a Somatron and the person who operates it has compiled three different tapes for music listening:

- Himalayan Bells II
- *Halpern's* Spectrum Suite *and Yogananda's* Divine Gypsy
- *Classical music of Ravel; Respighi's* The Pines of Rome, *and Debussy's* Girl with Flaxen Hair

Western classical music tends to have too much of a "tension and resolution" pattern in it for purposes of deep relaxation. That is, passages build up in intensity and draw the listener's anticipation, then drop the emotion, then build up again, so a continual pattern is created of tense anticipation. However, it is useful in providing guided imagery experiences when a structure is given by the facilitator. Classical music from the impressionist period can be used because it contains flowing patterns rather than dramatic build-up-and-release patterns.

New Age music tends to leave the listener free to create his/her own images, and the body free to choose its own rhythm. There are long, resonating tones, a drone background with little harmonic movement, and slow revolving melodies, so that tones "sink in." New Age music has repetitions in harmony, timbre, and melody which allow the listener to relax effortlessly and create a personal inner experience.

In contrast, Elgar's *Enigma Variations No. 8 and 9* entrains the mind to follow the melodies, which change and carry one up and down the scale, thus one stays in a more conscious state where the rational mind operates in structure and analysis.

Synthesized music: works well on the Somatron because the electronic sound picks up well in the bass. A lot of New Age music is synthesized. There is a certain fullness, a kind of kinetic feeling, fostered by synthesized music. The body can really feel the vibrations.

Vocals: are a little muffled on the Somatron. If vocals are used it is better to have words in a different language so one hears mostly the tones and vowels of the words instead of having to focus on the meaning of the words which draws one away.

Gregorian chant: has long drone all the way through but on the Somatron this sound is too much of the same tone for most people. Therefore it would be better to use the chant for only a few moments and add other types of music to the experience.

Ambient (nature) sounds: work well on the Somatron. Sometimes it is good to start a listening session with ocean waves, bird sounds, or wind to help the listener relax in preparation for deep listening.

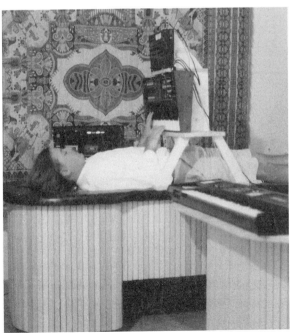

Composing music on the Somatron.

103

Playing live music through the Somatron is most effective. A musician in Tampa, Florida, set up keyboard instruments around the Somatron table and plugged them directly into the table. He produced recordings (not for sale commercially). The effectiveness of his music is due to the fact that the musician was lying on the table while he created the music spontaneously.

Several other musicians connecting the harp to the Somatron have achieved dramatic effects. Several harpists, including Sara Jane Williams (author of *The Mythic Harp* and *Harp Therapy Journal*) does a work she calls "Vibroacoustic Therapy" with her concert harp connected to the Somatron.

Somatron vibroacoustic products include a large number of chairs, pillows, mats, and beds utilizing their technology.[14]

---

[14] Somatron vibroacoustic products are sold by the manufacturer, Byron Eakin, in Tampa, Florida. For a complete product list and details, see their Web site: www.Somatron.com.

CHAPTER 9

Toward a New Science of Music

*Music is . . . a labyrinth with no beginning
and no end, full of new paths to discover,
where mystery remains eternal.*

PIERRE BOULEZ

Walt Whitman said, "Music is what awakens in us when reminded by the instruments." This conveys the essence of the answer to the question, "Why use music in healing?" For it is our own healing energies that awaken in us when reminded by the instruments. The whole universe is one great symphony and everything in it resonates to that symphony, in its own frequency. We create cacophony and dissonance in our bodies and in life around us when we do not experience this harmony.

Music is holistic, as it affects the body in many ways. When the music begins, the body listens. When we relearn how to hear again, through the introduction of beautiful harmonies of music and sound, we are ultimately drawn deeply into our very center and, once again, manifest our lives in harmony with the greater whole. In music lies the power to complete the great circle of the evolution of human consciousness.

We have two aspects to study in regard to using music in healing: soothing and stirring up. It is not as simple as some writers would have us believe. We are rediscovering an ancient knowledge that was passed from one priest to another in centuries past, although many ancient writings are too general to be of much use. Randall McClellan, music educator, composer, and writer, in a talk presented at the Music and Health Conference at Eastern Kentucky University in 1987, "Educating Music and Health Practitioners," said:

> It is the destiny of future generations of musicians to rediscover the ancient laws and develop a practice of music which will harmonize, integrate, and heal by means of a deeper understanding of vibration and its effect upon the body, mind, and soul of mankind. Music creates its own reality of time/space through the flow of kinetic energy, which it generates. It is kinetic energy made audible that effects changes in perception through its influence on human consciousness of creator and listener alike.

McClellan proposed four progressive steps in the task of creating a new science of music in healing for the future:

Collect and catalog the mythologies and legends that pertain to past use of music within healing contexts. Connect with other fields such as historical researchers who study past uses of music healing (anthropologists, musicologists, shamans, and neurologists in brain study) and then cross-reference the studies.

Establish research centers that combine therapies that use various aspects of vibration. Here, music researchers might collaborate with specialists in color therapy, ultrasonic, chromatics, flower essence therapy, polarity therapy, and bioacoustics. Psychologists, nutritionists, psychophysical practitioners, and spiritual advisors who develop a holistic approach to health that addresses all aspects of the human condition could enhance this work.

Develop a new form of pan-cultural music that combines rhythm, melody, tempo, drones, and ostinatoes for specific thera-peutic purposes. Perhaps a new ritual of performance will emerge here. Specially designed environments would utilize music, color, scents, and movements which coordinate healing, relaxation, medi-tation, and aesthetic enjoyment.

The development of a curriculum for the training of music healing practitioners, so in the future their services will be ordered by music prescription.

New Programs

Music as an enhancing agent in the healing process has been given a new direction in the music practitioner programs that began in the 1990s. Whereas traditional music therapy is an accepted professional field with accrediting programs of study established at many colleges and universities, this new accredited branch of healing with music has become available for those who seek practical skills for more holistic approaches to music as a healing agent.

Music Therapists[15] are trained and certified to do interactive therapies with patients, working in groups to do rhythmic exercises for neurological stimulation and also to participate in singing or musical activity for socialization. Certified Music Practitioners are not trained to do interactive therapies. They are to provide live music for the purpose of contributing to a healing environment at the bedside, often in situations where the patients may be too ill to communicate. Musicians play for the dying, hospital recovery, neo-natal wards, nursing homes, and other institutions.

Presently, there are four related programs in the United States.

---

[15] For further information, see www.musictherapy.org.

For the most part graduates are harpists, though other instruments are played.

Music for Healing and Transition: This program prepares musicians to serve the ill and/or the dying and all those who may benefit by being provided with live music to create a healing environment. Students are trained to play in the background quietly. The majority of students play the harp but other musical instruments, including voice, are accepted.

International Harp Therapy: Interactive program; practitioners can recognize certain signs in patients. Very specific music (the modes). Students interact with the patient, letting them actually hold and play small lap harps.

The Chalice of Repose: An intense, passive, highly trained, directed program. Consists mostly of Early Music or the modes; used as a bridge for the dying. Usually uses two harpists playing at the same time by the bedside.

Healing Harps: Students learn to work directly with people with physical ailments to affect their health. Uses the harp as an individual healing tool. Patients are disabled, challenged by chronic health problems. When the harps are played the pain may diminish or go away completely.

The courses include training in diverse subjects, such as repertoire development, with specific styles and rhythm to play for individuals according to their situations; etiquette in the hospital; diseases and pharmacology; care of the dying; understanding hospital equipment and procedures; understanding current medical issues; how music heals; and also injury prevention for the harpists, teaching them how to hold their instruments.

We are at a notable time in music history when there is an incredible variety of sound available. There is a fusing of cultures, new combinations of instruments playing together, and new synthesizers, tone generators, and technology. Hundreds of new recordings come out every year. The recognition that music and sound have the power to create the healing state or cause disharmony as well, is a catalyst to the creation of many challenging questions. A continuation of the research effort will lead to definite results over the years to come. It is believed that brain research will be a leading field to give us answers to the questions we have in many areas of music healing.

There are a number of musicians who compose music specifically for healing. This music actually started in the1960s with American composers in New York such as Terry Riley and Philip Glass. The style was named "minimal" or atonal music. It is characterized by a repetition of short motifs, which alter imperceptibly and vary only minimally. The music is composed in a state of constant regeneration so that a continuous flow of sound is heard.

Through a successive superimposition of minute figures with just one sustaining note, the sound of overtones (resonating multidimensional sounds that originate from a single note), movement and non-movement dissolves into a synchronicity. At first this may sound monotonous but the more one listens to it the more one feels a deep self-experience.

Two musicians come to mind when I think of music specifically composed intuitively for healing.

Herb Ernst, composer and musician living in the north Georgia mountains, composed three CDs, *Dreamflight Trilogy,* over a period of four years from 1986 to 1990[16] which he has written about extensively on his Web site. Herb says:

> To me, "intuitive music" is music that has, at its core, inspiration from one's Inner, or Higher Self. It is not a mental construct. I

---

[16] See Appendix 2: Tonal Symbols of Intuitive Music.

believe that intuitive music, in its purest state, can be recognized by simple but elegant harmonies and clear, open "cleansing" timbres. I try to become sensitive to the Highest while in a meditative state, to the Source of All Being. No other "disembodied entities" are involved.

[Trilogy] is a collection of music whose themes were derived while I was in a meditative state, and were played in their entirety only once, without composition or rehearsal . . . most music, when it came to me, had with it a visual image of personal, emotional content.

Rusty Crutcher, who created Emerald Green Sound Productions, composes music from sounds he hears in sacred sites. He goes to a place and listens not only to audible outer sounds, but also to the more subtle inner sounds of the place. Then he goes back to his studio with a "sketch recording" and creates music to go with what he picked up.

Musician and writer Peter Michael Hamel says, "Once we stop listening in terms of 'right or wrong,' and really listen to these unfamiliar intervals for what they are, they are the very ones that import to us a deep new experience" (Hamel 1978). To be able to listen to these new sounds without judgment or comparison, to surrender to the music, brings one to a new direction, and new ideas will flow into the mind and life experience.

What Is Healing Music?

Four music composers: Dr. Steven Halpern, a recognized pioneer in the field of contemporary music composition and sound and health; Don Campbell, music educator, author, and world traveler; Kay Gardner (1941–2002), music educator, teacher, author, and lecturer; and Tom Kenyon, psychoacoustic brain researcher, musician, and teacher, have their own views of what comprises healing music.

Halpern: His major aim is to produce music that is therapeutic, and to do so all semblance of a regular beat is removed in his compositions. He says this leaves spaces between the musical phrases and allows the meditative mood to develop, thereby increasing the theta brain wave pattern (deep relaxation) in the listener.

Campbell: Says it takes from five to seven minutes to begin to feel the space of music. This "space" in the musical design is important. He feels the musical environment where healing occurs is created due to the texture and patterning of the music, the time of day one listens, the attitude and the environment. Campbell says one tone prolonged in the lower ranges is important for healing music, a repeated motif, and not too much repetition so it does not become boring. All these qualities make up the power of music to soothe or stir up.

Gardner: Says there are basically nine elements in composing healing music:

1. *Intent:* the most important. The composer must have the intention to create healing music; immerse himself/herself in pure, loving thought, and open to the Divine.

2. *Drone:* long, uninterrupted sounds (such as in East Indian ragas) which set up a sympathetic vibration.

3. *Repetition:* to establish a tone of comfort and familiarity.

4. *Harmonics:* overtones, the spiritual content in music.

5. *Harmony:* simple, the emotional content.

6. *Melody:* gives direction, takes you somewhere and transcends pain.

7. *Form:* gives direction.

8. *Instrumental color:* pertains to different instruments that affect different parts of the body. (See diagrams in Appendix 2.)

9. *Rhythm:* deep, healthy pulse must be achieved.

Kenyon: Uses the latest multi-track technology to create healing music that utilizes a combination of sixty beats per minute, rhythm, rocking motions, F-major chord called the "perfect harmonic fifth" as used in Greek Mystery Schools, subliminals using NLP (neurolinguistic programming), Ericksonian hypnotherapy metaphors, psychoacoustic frequencies that balance the brain waves, bells, keyboard vocals, and whale and dolphin sounds. These recordings, when scientifically tested on spectrum analysis machines show a very high frequency. They give full body information for the listener, with the intent to feed and nourish the endocrine and nervous systems of the body, heal memories, and stimulate profound states of relaxation and awareness.

It is interesting to note that our listening capacity is conditioned. We hear culturally, genetically, and according to what is in the individual memory. We listen, then link the pieces we know with given emotional, mental, or even unconscious associations. Nevertheless, there is a spiritual power to be felt in great works of music which may lead the listener into a whole new world of experience. A reminder, momentarily, of the larger picture in life, of restoration and harmony.

AFTERWORD

The work I have done in music healing has been personally fulfilling and has affirmed my feeling from childhood that sound (hearing) is one of the more important aspects of human growth. I have gone from listening deeply to the sounds of nature, to hearing music and sound through the latest technologies.

Jane Roberts, author, has said it most succinctly in her book, *Nature of Personal Reality:*

> Technology brings within your search the great therapy of music; this activates the inner living cells of your body, stimulates the energy of the inner self and helps to unite the conscious mind with the other portions of your being. Music is an exterior representation and an excellent one, of the life-giving inner sounds that act therapeutically within your body all the time. The music is a conscious reminder of those deeper rhythms, both of sound and of motion. Listening to music that you like will often bring images into your mind that show you your conscious beliefs in different form.

We access in music what we need, what may be missing in our own voice, our own life. In the same manner, blocked areas in the physical body such as the heart, lungs, and joints, can be gently opened through music that we hear at the right moment. In the same way, music can gently open unspoken thoughts deep inside. And music can provide for us frequencies we do not naturally generate. There are sometimes archetypes heard in great music. These are pure tones going beyond the mass mind of humanity, and outside the matrix of human thought.

This book has documented the early years of my work in studying the vibration of music, but it only scratches the surface of what I have learned. It will require another book to bring this to light. It is hoped this first book will be of benefit to those who have not looked into the subject before, and inspire them to listen more consciously to the music all around us.

Appendix 1

METHODS OF UTILIZING
PRESCRIPTIVE SOUND

METHOD	HEALING APPROACH	CRITERIA FOR MUSIC SELECTION	FORM USED
Guided Imagery and Music(GIM)	Psychotherapeutic, accessing material from deep unconscious mind. Spontaneous images and feeling from childhood events may surface in a context that promotes positive experience. Deep listening in an altered state. Listener lies on a couch or table, works with a "guide" who is trained in this method.	Classical music* 1. Must engage listener immediately. 2. Has variety and shape. 3. Structure and form well-integrated with clearly focused moods. 4. Consistency in energy (no abrupt mood changes). 5. Compatible in instrumentation. 6. No redundant repetitions. 7. Compatible ending selection that produces nurturing affect. 8. Balance in music elements (pitch, rhythm, melody, harmony, timbre, vocal/ instrumental mood). 9. Directionality to move listener forward in the mind-processing. 10. Each selection no longer than 20 minutes each on the tape. *(Keiser, 1979)*	Specially designed tape recordings of classical music only. Contain four to six different selections. Each tape has six stages: Pre-onset Onset Build to a peak Peak Stabilization Return

APPENDIX 1—*Methods of Utilizing Prescriptive Sound cont.*

METHOD	HEALING APPROACH	CRITERIA FOR MUSIC SELECTION	FORM USED
The Tomatis Method— "Audio- Psychophonology" (APP)	Auditory stimulation, which assists and accelerates the development of listening skills, language and communication. By retraining the listening, via high-frequency audition, stuttering, dyslexia, depressions and many other psychological and neurological disorders are corrected. A series of listening sessions over a period of about four months are given. It also increases body awareness, builds body image, and promotes better awareness of space/time. The Mother's voice, when it is available, is added to the filtered music in the first phase.	**Mozart music,** believed to achieve balance with relaxing and energizing effects. Most feature violin, as in symphonies, serenades, divertimentos and concertos. **Gregorian chant,** which has a relaxing, peaceful rhythm, and rich, timberous overtones from 2000 to 4000 hz. **Children's songs and nursery rhymes** harmonize body movements and motor functions by affecting the vestibular system of the ear.	"Electronic Ear" machine, connected with a set of head phones, a micro-phone, and certain filters which together are a working model of the human ear.

* FDA regulations forbid making claims of healing with these instruments. This label is my recommendation personally.

APPENDIX 1—*Methods of Utilizing Prescriptive Sound cont.*

METHOD	HEALING APPROACH	CRITERIA FOR MUSIC SELECTION	FORM USED
Psychoacoustic "Betar" instrument	**Transformational,** * a sound velocity of 85 decibels is experienced throughout the body. This powerful sound, with the addition of subliminal sound frequencies will bring to the listener a great release. This method gives the listener approximately a 45 min. experience.	The listener selects specific pieces of music he or she relates to, and these selections are used in the beginning. Every kind of music is used: Rock, Classical, Country Western, New Age, Ethnic, Show Tune, Vocal, Instrumental, Chant, and Ambient (nature) sound. "Intution " is basis of music selections, and subliminals. The facilitator makes and cues music selections, and controls a mixer, volume levels, and monitors the listener.	Giant sized geodesic structure with floating center table. Music operation is located in a panel nearby with stereo state-of-the art equipment and laser compact discs of music are played.A holographic bubble of sound is created; creating a feeling of being "inside" sound.
"Somatron" stereophonic music table.	Vibro-tactile stimulation which bathes the listener at a cellular level. Uses are many: massage, guided imagery, stress release, Chiropractic treatments, physical fitness centers, peak performance athletes, mental institutions, etc.	Depending upon its many uses, music selection fairly wide, except: music with constant bass repetition not effective, due to the table's propensity to accentuate low bass tones.	Soft, padded table with 8 speakers enclosed. Stereo component with CD or tape cassette capability, with 7 band equalizer. Transmits hundreds of vibrating frequencies to match the music simultaneously.

* *FDA regulations forbid making claims of healing with these instruments. This label is my recommendation personally.*

Appendix 2
TONAL SYMBOLS OF INTUITIVE MUSIC

SOUND	ARCHETYPAL SYMBOL
Harp	Simplicity; Purity; "Return to the Source"; Eternal, Original Vibration or Power Sound (i. e., "The Word")
Soaring/Shimmering Strings	Radiating Vital Life Force; the Aura; Streaming Thought Energy; Flowing Emotions Such as Love
Chimes and Bells	Focused/Directed Thought Energy; Manifestation; Clarity; Concentrated Vital Life Force; Affirmations, Goals; Achievements
Brass Horns	Spiritual Awakening; Masculine Power
Reed Instruments	Vulnerability; Quiet Inner Strength
Flutes	Nurturing; Gentleness; Openness; Healing; Feminine Energy
Drums/	Power, Strength; Heartbeat; Life
Choir	Angelic Presences and Forces; The Higher Self; Heaven
Cathedral Organ	"The Voice of God"
Ascending Scales and Arpeggios	Uplifting of Consciousness; Cosmic Attunement; Energy Transfers from Physical World to Spiritual World
Descending Scales and Arpeggios	Influx of Divine Power into Matter and/or Humanity

SOUND	ARCHETYPAL SYMBOL
Minor Scales & Chords	Introspection; "Centering"; "Processing"; Feminine Receptivity; Dissolution; "Negative" Polarity of the Universe
Major Scales& Chords	Expansion of Consciousness; Spiritual Empowerment; Feminine and Masculine Creation; "Positive" Polarity of the Universe
Trills	Cosmic Vibrations; Universal Energy
Water Sounds	Stream of Consciousness
Wind Sounds	Astral Flight; Freedom of the Soul or Spirit
Reverberation and Echo Effects	Limitlessness of Space, Time and Consciousness
Tempo Acceleration	Quickening of Awareness; Making Physical, Mental, Emotional, Psychic or Spiritual "Connections"; Manipulation of Time Waves (e. g., Going so Fast that Everything Seems to Stop)
Tempo Deceleration	Merging with Universal Consciousness; Manipulation of Time Waves (e. g., Going so Slow that Everything Seems to Stop)

Appendix 3

BODY RHYTHMS/PULSES

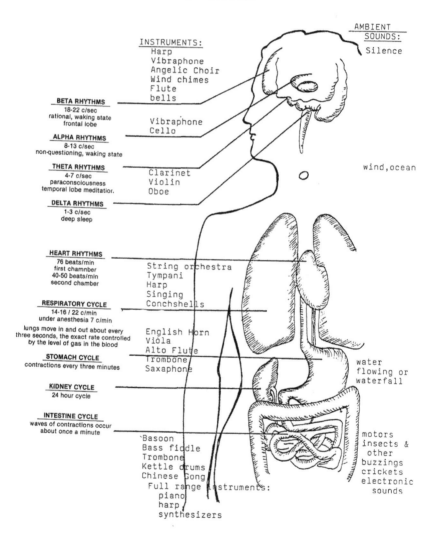

AMBIENT SOUNDS:

INSTRUMENTS:
Harp
Vibraphone
Angelic Choir
Wind chimes
Flute
bells

Silence

BETA RHYTHMS
18-22 c/sec
rational, waking state
frontal lobe

Vibraphone
Cello

ALPHA RHYTHMS
8-13 c/sec
non-questioning, waking state

THETA RHYTHMS
4-7 c/sec
paraconsciousness
temporal lobe meditatior.

Clarinet
Violin
Oboe

wind, ocean

DELTA RHYTHMS
1-3 c/sec
deep sleep

HEART RHYTHMS
76 beats/min
first chamnber
40-50 beats/min
second chamber

String orchestra
Tympani
Harp
Singing
Conchshells

RESPIRATORY CYCLE
14-16 / 22 c/min
under anesthesia 7 c/min

lungs move in and out about every
three seconds, the exact rate controlled
by the level of gas in the blood

English Horn
Viola
Alto Flute

STOMACH CYCLE
contractions every three minutes

Trombone
Saxaphone

water
flowing or
waterfall

KIDNEY CYCLE
24 hour cycle

INTESTINE CYCLE
waves of contractions occur
about once a minute

Basoon
Bass fiddle
Trombone
Kettle drums
Chinese Gong
Full range instruments:
piano
harp
synthesizers

motors
insects &
other
buzzings
crickets
electronic
sounds

Appendix 4

Suggested form for clients to fill out in preparation for sound therapy. It is confidential and to be used only as a reference point for the therapist.

SOUND THERAPY QUESTIONNAIRE

Date _____

Name _____

Birth date _____

Address _____

Phone (Home) _____(Work) _____

Current family structure _____

Spiritual system you work with _____

Other therapies you have worked with; with whom? _____

Do you recall your dreams (night), record them . . . work with them?

Are you sensitive to color? _____

Medical and health problems _____

SOUND THERAPY QUESTIONNAIRE *(page two)*

Emotional experiences or traumatic physical experiences you have had in your
life (accidents, surgery, shock) _____

_____

_____

Reason for your coming _____

_____

Goals you have for yourself? _____

_____

Current source of emotional support _____

_____

Current profession or work _____

_____

Music background and/or special experiences with sound _____

_____

Any other comments you feel might be helpful to me in helping you

_____

_____

_____

_____

_____

_____

_____

_____

_____

_____

_____

References

Abel, Arthur. *Talks with Great Composers*. London and New York: Theosophical Press, 1987.

Bentov, Itzhak. *Stalking the Wild Pendulum*. 2nd ed. New York: Inner Traditions, 1988.

Bonny, Helen L. *The Role of Taped Music Programs in the GIM Process: Theory and Product—Monograph 2*. Baltimore: 1978.

————. "Music, the Language of Immediacy," paper for National Conference of Art Therapies Association. Seattle: 1985.

Bonny, Helen L. and Louis M. Savory. *Music and Your Mind: Listening with a New Consciousness*. New York: 1973.

Campbell, Don. *Introduction to the Musical Brain*. St. Louis: 1984.

Clynes, Manfred. *Sentics: The Touch of the Emotions*. Garden City, NY: 1978.

Cook, Pat Moffit. *Shaman, Ihankri and Nele, Music Healers of Indigenous Cultures* (book and CD). New York: Ellipsis Arts, 1998.

Critchley, M., M.D., and R. A. Henson. *Music and the Brain: Studies in the Neurology of Music*. Springfield, IL: 1977.

Dunne, Claire, *Carl Jung, Wounded Healer of the Soul*. New York: Parabola Books, 2000.

Diamond, John, M.D. *The Life Energy in Music*. Vol. 2. New York: 1983.

Gardner, Kay. *Sounding the Inner Landscape: Music Medicine*. Stonington, ME: Cadeuceus Publishers, 1990.

Garfield, Leah Maggie. *Sound Medicine*. CA: 1987.

Gillmore, Tim and Paul Madaule. *The Tomatis Anthology* Canada: 1988.

Gillmore, Tim; Paul Madaule; and Billie Thompson. *About the Tomatis Method*. Canada: 1988.

Goldman, Jonathan. *Awakening the Lost Chord*. Boston: 1984.

Gundling, Dorothy, Ph.D., *Breaking the Silence*. Kearney, NE: Morris Publishing, 1998.

Hamel, Peter M. *Through Music to the Self: How to Appreciate and Experience Anew*. England: Vega Books, 2002.

Harvey, Arthur. "Music and Health," *International Brain Dominance Review Newsletter,* Lake Lure, NC: 1987.

Harvey, Arthur; Ole Anderson; and Marcy Marsh. *Learn with the Classics.* San Francisco: The Lind Institute, 1999.

Houston, Jean. *The Search for the Beloved.* Los Angeles: J. P. Tarcher, 1987.

Hunt, Valerie. *Infinite Mind.* Malibu, CA: Malibu Publications, 1984.

———. *Mind Mastery Meditations.* Malibu, CA: Malibu Publications, 1997.

Joudry, Patricia. *Sound Therapy for the Walkman.* Canada: 1984.

Katie, Byron. *Loving What Is,* New York: Harmony Books, 2002.

Khan, Pir Inayat. *Music.* New Delhi, India: Sufi Publishing Company, 1962.

Keiser, Linda H. *Conscious Listening: Annotated Guide to the ICM Taped Music Programs.* Baltimore: 1986.

Leuner, Dr. Hans Carl. "Guided Affective Imagery (GAI)," *American Journal of Psychotherapy.* Vol. 23, 1969.

Madaule, Paul. "Listening in the Story of Your Life," from Life in Motion—The Body/Mind Connection Conference, New York University, 1989.

McClellan, Randall. *The Healing Forces of Music.* Warwick, NY: 1988.

McKinney, Cathy. "The Effect of Music on Imagery," *American Journal of Music Therapy,* 27(1), 1990, p. 34.

McKinney, Maria DeRungs, DMA. *The Healing Tones of Music.* Everett, WA: Casa de Maria Research Center, 1986.

Pert, Candice. *Molecules of Emotion: The Science Behind Mind-Body Medicine.* New York: Simon & Shuster, 1999.

Rosenfeld, A. "Music, the Beautiful Disturber," *Psychology Today.* Dec. 1985, 48–56.

Rosenstiel, Leonie, ed. *Shirmer History of Music.* New York: Shirmer Books, 1982.

Savory, Louis and Linda Albert. *Welcome to the Somatron Experience.* Florida: 1987.

Tame, David. The Secret Power of Music. New York: Destiny Books, 1984.

Tomatis, A. A., M.D. 1972 Newsletter, Sound Listening Center, Phoenix, AZ.

———. 1988 Newsletter, Sound Listening Center, Phoenix, AZ.

———. *The Conscious Ear.* New York: Station Hill Press, 1991.

Van Dusen, Wilson. *The Natural Depth in Man.* New York: Harper & Row, 1981, 1990.

———. *Beauty, Wonder, and the Mystical Mind.* Pennsylvania: Chrysilis Books, Swedenborg Foundation, 1999.

Weeks, Bradford. *The Therapeutic Effect of High Frequency Audition.* 1987.

Illustrations

COVER
Alana Woods, photograph by Jonathan Lowe.

FRONT MATTER
Dove Logo, drawn by author.

CHAPTER 1
Two harpists, from *Music: A Pictorial Archive of Woodcuts & Engravings,* copyright-free illustrations.

Harpist and chirononomist, 5th Dynasty, courtesy of Lise Manniche, *Music and Musicians in Ancient Egypt,* British Museum Press, 1991.

CHAPTER 2
Flutist playing for children, from *Music: A Pictorial Archive of Woodcuts & Engravings,* copyright-free illustrations.

CHAPTER 3
Standard cycle of emotions (from music therapy notes).

Arrangement of adjectives (from music therapy notes).

Six Greek Modes, courtesy of P. D. Costello Publications, Santa Cruz, California, 1983.

CHAPTER 4
Diagram of the brain, *The Brain, a User's Manual,* The Diagram Group.

CHAPTER 6
Diagram of the Electronic Ear, drawing.

Harpist playing lyre, from *Music: A Pictorial Archive of Woodcuts & Engravings,* copyright-free illustrations.

CHAPTER 7
Experiencing the Betar, author's photo.

CHAPTER 8
The Somatron Apollo, author's photo.

Composing music on the Somatron, author's photo.

APPENDICES
Appendix 1: Methods of Utilizing Prescriptive Sound, by Alana Woods.

Appendix 2: Tonal Symbols of Intuitive Music, by written permission, Herb Ernst.

Appendix 3: Diagram of Body Rhythms/ Pulses, credits: Derek and Julia Parker, *The Compleat Astrologer,* New York: 1971; Leah Maggie Garfield, *Sound Medicine,* California, 1987; Kay Gardner, 1984.

Appendix 4: Sound Therapy Questionnaire, by Alana Woods.

Index

All Children's Hospital 100
Alschuller/Iso 41,61
Ambient sounds 103
Ancients 27
Asclepius 29
Asia 20
Autism 12, 81

Bali 20-21
Balinese 20
Betar 53, 84-93
Birdsong 41
Body 44-50
Bombay 22
Bonny, Helen 16, 55-69
Brain 45

Campbell, Don 20, 111
Caruso 73
Caves 22, 23
Chant 77-78, 103
Childhood 17, 41
Children's songs 77
Classical 57
Clynes 37
Cook, Pat Moffit 22
Composing 103, 109
Cortical Charge 79
Crutcher, Rusty 110

Disease 34

Eastern Kentucky
    University 46
Eakin, Byron 94
Edison Dev. Center 100

Electronic Ear 71
Emotional 35
Emotions 35-40
Endorphins 47
Entrainment 94
Epidarus 28
Ernst, Herb 109-110
Evolution 69

Gamelon 20
Gardner, Kay 11, 20, 110
Geodesic dome 84
GIM 53-69
Greece 21, 28, 30, 33, 94
Gregorian 103
Groff, Stan 55

Halpern, Steven 110-111
Harp 19, 27
Harvey, Arthur 46
Healing 53
Healing centers 106-107
Healing Harps 108
Hearing 3, 72, 82
Henson 48
Hevner 37
Holistic 32-34
Holistic music 105
Holographic 92-93
Hunt, Valerie 38-39

Imagery 63
Imaginal realm 48
India 22
International Harp

Therapy 108
Intuitive music 109

Jung, Carl 53

Katie, Byron 34
Kelly, Peter 84
Kenyon, Tom 43, 112
Kinetic 91, 95

Limbic system 47
Listening 72,73, 82
Listening Center 81
Lullabies 79
Lydian Mode 58

Madaule, Paul 76
Memory states 63
McClellan, Randall 27, 106,
    107
Modes 39
Mood states 38
Mozart 77
Multi-purpose table 95
Music practitioners 42-107
Music selection 89, 96
Music therapists 41, 107

NASA 101
Nature 18, 23
Neurophysiological 18, 82
New Age music 90, 102
New programs 107
New sounds 109

Pan-cultural 107

Paracelsus 21
Piano 17
Plato 33
Practitioner 42
Precautions 92
Psychoacoustic 84
Pythagoras 27, 28

Research 100
Roberts, Jane 113

Savory, Louis 16
Selection of music 96
Sentic forms 37
Somatron 53, 94, 104
Sound 108
Sound therapy 35
Sperry, Roger 46
Storytelling 19
Stress release 92
Subliminals 88
Symphony 15
Synthesized music 102

Temples 28, 29
Therapist 42
Tingklik 20
Tomatis, A. A. 70-83
Tomita 17

Ubud 20

Vibroacoustic therapy 104

Western classical music
  102

Workshops 41

ORDER FORM

Stay in touch

The following materials are available to order:

The Healing Touch of Music: An Exploration *Book — with accompanying CD.*	$21.95
Music to Heal the Family Soul *CD — Solo harp.*	$15.95
The Sound of Healing *Video (VHS) — A practical documentary that demonstrates toning in an ancient cave, the use of music in dentistry, working with music and a mentally retarded child, and historical uses of music.*	$24.95
The Little Alabaster Box *Cassette — A story with harp soundtrack.* *Hidden truth that expands with each listening.*	$11.95
Shipping & handling to U.S., Mexico & Canada *($5.00 for 1 item; $7.50 for 2 to 5 items)*	

Group discounts of 20% per order of 5 or more of any item.
Please make check payable in U.S. dollars to Alana Woods.

SOUND
VISTAS
P.O. Box 20471
Albuquerque, NM 87154-0471
E-mail: alanawoods@earthlink.net
Web: www.soundvistas.com